SUCCESSFUL
COLD
BUFFETS

PETER GROTZ

SUCCESSFUL
COLD
BUFFETS

FOREWORD BY

RAYMOND BLANC

 VAN NOSTRAND REINHOLD
_____ New York

About the Author

Peter Grotz is Head Chef at the Frankfurt Airport Steigenberger Hotel. He is a master in producing decorative dishes which are both varied and visually perfect. Throughout his career he has specialised in the art of the Cold Buffet, constantly refining and perfecting his work. In two recent Culinary Olympics at Frankfurt he has won gold medals for his cold dishes. He has been a working chef since 1969.

Contents

Foreword by Raymond Blanc

Books specialising in buffets are very tempting to buy. A great deal of money is often lavished upon the presentation and cosmetics, with page after page of glossy photographs. Unfortunately, more often than not, a pretty picture book is produced which has little or no use to the amateur or professional, and all too often it finds its way onto the coffee table or bookshelf, only to gather dust. The emphasis is on cosmetics only, with the result that the seemingly perfect displayed dishes, highly coloured, masked with perfect transparent jelly, are totally unedible.

By contrast however, I find SUCCESSFUL COLD BUFFETS to be both stimulating and clear to the reader. Many of these attractive recipes could be followed by the amateur; the colour photography is excellent and the many colour pictures are always relevant to the text and will help enormously in the explanation of the recipe itself.

I also enjoyed the content of this book because it has an honest approach and encapsulates today's cuisine. There is a definite order; the cosmetic make-up is not to the detriment of the quality of the food, and the care which

is taken to build up taste and texture is significant. The author has made this highly skilled and elitist subject more attainable to all of us by simplifying and removing the affectation of the buffet.

Consequently I am sure that many of these delightful and novel canapés and dishes will soon be increasingly in demand and in use in hotels and restaurants, and indeed in private homes, wherever this book is available. I raise a glass to the success of SUCCESSFUL COLD BUFFETS!

Reginald Blau.

Glossary

The following terms and expressions may be helpful to the reader.

Best end	(of veal, lamb etc.) – A joint of veal or lamb consisting of several chops or cutlets together (a "rack")
Capsicums	Bell Peppers
Clingfilm	Saran wrap (U.S.A.)
Couverture	A prepared chocolate used by pastry cooks for multi-purpose uses, such as fillings, icings etc.
Double cream	Heavy cream
Kenya beans	These are an extremely thin variety of green bean rather like a "bobby" bean, but about one third of the diameter. Most of those supplied in Europe, come by air from Kenya, hence the name
Pike-perch	A European fresh-water fish, also known as the zander or sander
Prove	To allow a yeast dough to double its size in a warm environment
Refresh	Shock (of boiled vegetables)
Serving dish	Any suitable service piece
Spring onions	Scallions
Stoned olives	Pitted olives

Publisher's Preface

This book has been translated from the German and edited for the English language reader. We believe we have provided a unique insight into the skills of the cold buffet table, an art which has been so successfully perfected by the European chef.

Measures are shown in metric and imperial throughout, and where possible, British and American terminology has been used. Some of the items required in the original recipes may not easily be available outside Germany. Rather than suggesting substitutions, we have added explanatory notes where necessary. It is of course not essential to adhere to a particular product for any one recipe, since most of them may be used as a basis for others, using different ingredients which can be obtained locally.

We are delighted that Raymond Blanc was sufficiently impressed with this book that he agreed to write the Foreword to this edition.

We hope that chefs and cooks throughout the English-speaking world will find inspiration and ideas from the many recipes and colour plates in the pages that follow.

Presentation

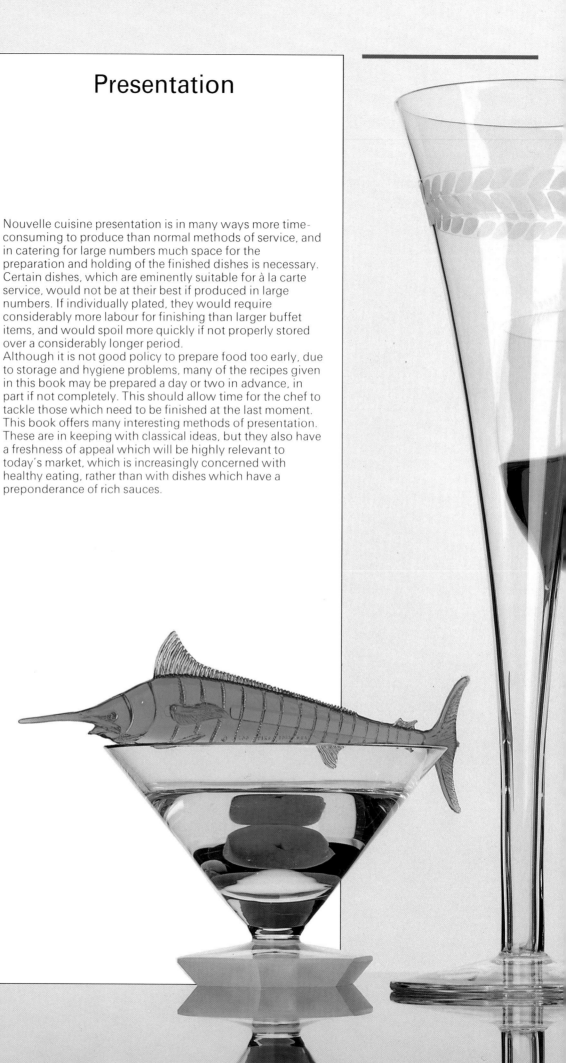

Nouvelle cuisine presentation is in many ways more time-consuming to produce than normal methods of service, and in catering for large numbers much space for the preparation and holding of the finished dishes is necessary. Certain dishes, which are eminently suitable for à la carte service, would not be at their best if produced in large numbers. If individually plated, they would require considerably more labour for finishing than larger buffet items, and would spoil more quickly if not properly stored over a considerably longer period.

Although it is not good policy to prepare food too early, due to storage and hygiene problems, many of the recipes given in this book may be prepared a day or two in advance, in part if not completely. This should allow time for the chef to tackle those which need to be finished at the last moment. This book offers many interesting methods of presentation. These are in keeping with classical ideas, but they also have a freshness of appeal which will be highly relevant to today's market, which is increasingly concerned with healthy eating, rather than with dishes which have a preponderance of rich sauces.

Buffet Drinks

Sufficient drinks of mixed types with their requisite glasses need to be readily available. Much will depend on the theme of the buffet, and on the aims and objectives of the organisers. Once the plans for the buffet have been finalised, a decision can be made as to the types of drinks to be served.

Many people today will not drink alcohol, particularly if they are driving. Therefore a selection of non-alcoholic drinks need to be supplied.

Ice buckets/ice boxes are essential for keeping drinks cool, particularly with an outdoor or off-premises buffet.

Buffet Planning

While the chef should be guided by the wishes of the organiser of a buffet as to menu content, he can nevertheless bring in his own ideas, if he thinks that the requested items will cause problems either in production or service.

CHECKLIST

Numbers
Budget
Menu
Cutlery
Crockery
Glasses
Table Cloths and Napery
Advance Food Ordering
Preparation of Dishes
Ice
Floral Arrangements

Costing

If cost is paramount, individually portioned items must be supplied, or in the case of meats to be carved, for a carver to be placed behind the buffet table to help the customer and to control portion size. Alternatively, for certain high cost items, plated service should be considered.

Buffets, if planned well, can be very successful. There is much more freedom of choice as to quantity and type of food to be eaten, and personal preferences can be indulged. However, at the end of the day they must make a profit, and this can only be achieved by a good flexible pricing policy and by accurate costing both of commodities and labour. The scope is almost boundless – limited only by cost factors, the availability of food stuffs, and the imagination of the chef.

The whole field of buffets presents the imaginative chef and the banqueting manager with the opportunity to offer the customer many different styles of meal. These can range from the most formal, to al fresco meals in the open air, with all the different seasonal, national and cultural themes available.

Just as a formal dinner or banquet needs meticulous planning, so too does the less formal buffet. Bear in mind that the buffet, by its very nature, can be arranged almost anywhere, but this may not necessarily be in the most convenient place for the production of high class food items. For this reason, careful advance planning and preparation is essential.

It is important to assess the number of different dishes required, and then to prepare a detailed work schedule in advance of the function. Make sure you have all the equipment necessary, and avoid last minute panics.

The successful buffet can be both profitable, and also a function which will bring praises and accolades to the chef. If, in military terms, ''time spent in reconnaissance is seldom wasted'', then for the chef, time spent in planning is absolutely essential.

Einladung

If the tables are not to be laid, then cutlery, serviettes and glasses should be placed ready on a separate table

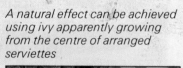

A natural effect can be achieved using ivy apparently growing from the centre of arranged serviettes

The Informal Buffet

The drinks are ready. Don't forget to supply corkscrews and bottle openers where necessary

The Italian Buffet

Illustration—Top left:
An Italian newspaper and serviettes in the Italian national colours help to make the spaghetti show up well in the glass container

Illustration—Bottom left:
The focal-point of the buffet: an original decoration consisting of spaghetti, tortellini, Italian flags, coloured ribbons and three-coloured noodles

Illustration—Right:
Striking swirls of coloured ribbon are placed between the dishes

The Festive Buffet

The use of paper doilies helps to make even small items like butter dishes interesting.

The bottom of the fruit basket should be padded out as a base, so that less fruit is needed to fill it.

Pyramids on which to place glasses can be easily made using various sizes of round boxes which are then covered with cloths or serviettes.

Work-plan for a Festive Buffet for 24 People

The following dishes have been offered:
Prime smoked fish dish with prawns and avocados,
horseradish cream and mustard and dill sauce (see p. 62)
Turbot stuffed with salmon (see p. 72)
Best end and medallions of veal with vegetable terrine (see p. 110)
Vegetable dish with basil and olive oil vinaigrette dressing (see p. 130)
French cheese selection with radishes and grapes (see p. 144)
Exotic fruit selection with Maraschino (see p. 158)
Selection of breads (see p. 156)

When date is fixed
Place hire order for tables, table linen, serviettes, glasses,
crockery and cutlery, if necessary from a specialist firm.

6 days before the party date
Order halibut, best end of veal and exotic fruits. Buy or
order the chosen drinks and have them delivered. Order the
floral decorations for buffet and tables.

5 days before the party date
Check the list of guests. Has anyone been missed out? Plan
the construction and placing of the buffet items.

4 days before the party date
Draw up the menu or menus and prepare the place cards, if
desired. Check availability of ice cube production for drinks
and cocktails, and make or order as necessary.
Order rolls and bread from baker, or make for freezing.

3 days before the party date
Check the availability of ordered items with suppliers in
order to change them, if unavailable.

2 days before the party date
Collect or have the previously ordered items delivered.
First food preparation tasks:
Bone, stuff and poach the halibut.
Roast the best end and fillet of veal.

1 day before the party date
Prepare all the items necessary for the cold dishes:
  Prepare the vegetable terrine and all the sauces.
  Finish off all the garnishes for the dishes, and the
  medallions of veal.
  Blanch the vegetables for the vegetable dish.
  Coat the halibut with the fish aspic jelly.
Polish and clean all serving dishes and coat them with aspic
if necessary.
If the room is available at this stage, put up the buffet table,
and tables for the guests and cloth them.
Lay out a table for the cutlery, serviettes and glasses.
Lay out service cutlery.
Arrange a base for the floral decoration, either using an
empty carton or a drinks case, clothed in a table cloth.

The day of the party
Ensure that all the drinks necessary are put to chill early,
either in the refrigerator, or in a bath of cold water with ice.
Prepare the fruit for the fruit platter and decorate the platter.
Finish off all the other dishes as necessary.
Collect or have the ordered bread delivered, or if frozen
bring out to thaw. Do not allow to dry out. Depending on
the types of bread, either cover with a moistened cloth, or
pass through a hot oven for a few minutes before serving.
Have the floral decorations delivered and decorate the
buffet and tables with them, as necessary.
Aim for everything to be ready at least three hours before
the arrival of the guests.
Check the buffet table against the plan to ensure that no
items have been forgotten.
During the meal, ensure that all used plates, cutlery and
glasses are removed.

Advice in Buying and Preparing

General

Although this present volume is intended for the professional chef, it will also have a place in the kitchen of those who are capable of more than basic cookery, and the following notes are intended for them as well as being perhaps a reminder to the professional, if one is needed. Quantities given in the recipes are for raw or unprepared items. In special cases, if it is necessary for the particular recipe, weights of cleaned or prepared items are given, for example if filleted fish or portioned meats are required. As the foodstuffs for a cold buffet are usually prepared 1 to 2 days in advance, it is essential that they are especially fresh when purchased. Check what is on offer and make comparisons. It is not always good policy to buy the cheapest. The best way is to purchase fruit, vegetables, fish or meat from specialist suppliers, who in many cases may help you to save time by undertaking some of the basic preparation, such as filleting of fish or boning of meat joints, poultry, etc.

The time thus saved can then be put to better use for other work.

Fish and Seafood

The purchase of smoked fish is relatively easy, but care must be taken that individual items, such as fillets of trout, mackerel, rollmops, etc. are all supplied in the same size to make for ease of decoration.

Smoked salmon can be purchased pre-sliced as it is difficult to slice for the non-professional and an effort must be made to ensure that all slices are the same size.

The purchase of fresh fish is somewhat more difficult. Great care must be taken to ensure the freshness of the fish and this can be done simply by checking a few details. The fish must be bright-eyed and have red gills. The flesh must be firm to the touch and a light thumb pressure should not leave a dent. The smell should be pleasant and not have any trace of ammonia. For fish with scales, these should be difficult to remove. Lastly, the fish should shine, not be slimy to the touch, and show no signs of external injury.

To poach fish, such as salmon, pike-perch or turbot, these should be placed into a cold cooking liquor and heated quickly to a point just under boiling-point when the heat should be reduced to allow for a slow poaching process. When the fish is cooked, it should be allowed to cool in the liquor until cold.

This will ensure that the flesh is succulent, and when cold will be easier to work on. In decorating slices of cooked fish, a thin coat of fish aspic will prevent drying out, and if shrimps, prawns, or other crustacea are used as a garnish, these also can be given a thin coat of fish aspic after putting in place.

Important points when buying fish: red gills and bright eyes

If contemplating preparation of the lobster dish, ensure that a pan large enough to take the lobster is to hand, and that the water is kept at a fast boil continuously.
The lobster should be put head-first into the boiling water and will change from the dark blue colour of the live lobster to the red typical of a cooked lobster.

Meat

First-class quality of all meat goods is equally important, especially in the case of pork goods, as there are so many differences in quality available.

Pork flesh should be pink with some fat running through it, and be lightly marbled. In this way, it will be succulent and tender when roasted.

Beef joints should appear dark red and likewise be marbled throughout the flesh. Joints, especially those used for roasting should be free from sinews, and the joints cut where possible so that there are no changes of direction of grain in the joint, in order to give a good appearance to the cut slices and make carving easier.

Veal should be a light pink colour and have hardly any fat, with the meat itself being very shiny. Calves' sweetbreads (thymus glands) are a speciality, and should be light pink to white in colour, with a firm consistency. They should be free from blood vessels, sinews and fat. Calves' sweetbreads must be well-rinsed before poaching, and scrupulously cleaned. Thus all bloody and gristly parts will be removed, leaving a light, almost white colour.

For the quality and flavour of the dishes it is especially important that the optimum cooking times are not exceeded, in order to keep the meat succulent and tender. When boiling meats the use of a meat thermometer will help to produce a well-cooked joint; beef should be cooked at between 60° and 70°C (140° and 158°F), veal and pork between 85° and 90°C (185° and 194°F).

Another means of testing is by using a trussing or larding needle. The needle is inserted into the meat to be tested and then withdrawn, when the end of it is placed between the tops of two adjoining fingers. In the case of veal and pork it should feel hot, but with beef it should only feel warm. This method can also be used to check cooking of game, poultry and fish, as well as pies and terrines. In these cases the needle should feel hot to the touch.

Roasted meats must be fully cooled, in the case of large joints, up to about 6 hours, before they are carved. In this fashion they will remain succulent without the juices running out. If carved too soon, the colour will deteriorate and the meat appear pale. In order that the slices will appear even when carved, the joints should be tied with string into the desired shape, before cooking.

Advice on Service

- Silver dishes can be protected from scratches and oxidation by coating them before use with a thin layer of clear aspic jelly. For meat dishes, this can be given a little colour by the addition of a little caramelised sugar.
- As a rule, fish and meat items should not be served on the same dishes, the only exception being in the case of canapés and appetisers.
- All garnishes used should be edible as a rule. Any inedible items such as paper decorations, streamers, ribbons etc. should be kept off the dishes themselves, the ground rule being that only edible items should be on the dishes of the buffet.
- Dishes should not be overloaded. It is important that guests can see quickly and easily what they are eating, especially in terms of garnish, eg, a whole filled cucumber. The edges of the dish must always be left clear.
- Similar items and garnishes belong together and should not be placed at random over the dish.

● Dishes which have been completed ready for service should be covered with clingfilm and kept in a cool place or chiller until required, provided they are not kept in too cold an area. They must not be allowed to freeze. In order that the clingfilm does not spoil any decoration or garnish, it should be kept off the actual surface of the food by using toothpicks as spacers, but these must be protected at the top ends in order not to pierce the clingfilm. Aluminium foil may be used instead, but care must be taken that it does not come into contact with any foods which are acid, or contain vinegar, as this will cause oxidation.

Poultry

Poultry is mainly sold deep-frozen, but for the preparation of cold dishes, fresh birds are preferable. It is important to check the quantity of meat on either side of the breastbone and on the legs.
Ducks have the best flavour when they are from 8 to 10 months old and have a weight of between 1.200 and 1.600 kilos ($3\frac{1}{2}$ and 4 lbs). Young birds can be recognised by their flexible breastbones.
Poulardes or fattened hens have a light, very succulent and tender flesh. The rib-cage is very flexible and soft.

Fattened hens (Poulardes) have especially tender flesh

Game

Rabbit should have a light pink colour and firm flesh. There should be no visible layer of fat. It should not be roasted too long, or it will become dry.
Hare will vary greatly according to age. The most flavoursome and tender flesh comes from hares of 4 to 8 months old. After this the flesh becomes mostly dry and tough. For roasting, the saddle fillets should be larded with strips of bacon, or if being used for hare pie, wrapped in fresh green (unsmoked) bacon, in order that the flesh remains moist.
Venison (Deer meat) is dark red. Animals with the best flavour are no more than 3 years old. Older animals have stringy meat and develop a very strong flavour.

Cold Meats, Sausages and Hams

It is important when buying cold meats, sausages and hams not to have the slices cut too thin, as they will hold better on the dish and after some time will not have a "tired" look.
For those dishes requiring lamb-, wild-boar- or venison-ham, these should be pre-ordered from your supplier to ensure their availability for the date in question.
If these items are required for a mixed dish of cold meats, then it is better to choose 2 smaller pieces than 1 larger one, as they will require less cooking time, and are easier to handle afterwards, in general smaller slices being easier to arrange on a dish than large ones.
Because of the large variety of sausage and ham specialities which exist, space does not allow for a full review, but it must always be borne in mind when dealing with an informal themed buffet to use items coming from a particular region. Be guided in the main by your supplier.

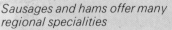

Sausages and hams offer many regional specialities

Fruit and Vegetables

Fruit may be used as a garnish for many dishes

In many dishes, fruit and vegetables are used as garnish or for decoration, and for this purpose if possible, whole, even-sized items should be used.

It is important when buying fruit to ensure that it is not bruised. Vegetables must be crisp and appear fresh. Salads should show no wilted leaves on the outside. Firm-leaved salad varieties will hold up better on display, and rather than use ordinary lettuce, lollo rosso, batavia, iceberg, curly endive, or chicory should be used. For those dishes where, in general, blanched vegetables are used, care must be taken that they are not left too long in the boiling water before refreshing in ice-cold water, in order to retain their crispness. It is better to under-blanch than over-blanch. Fruit should neither be bought over-ripe or under-ripe, and care must be taken with apples, pears, and bananas if these are displayed peeled, that they are well-sprinkled with lemon juice, in order that they do not go brown. Apples and pears may be lightly blanched in lemon water to which a little sugar has been added.

Cheeses

It could truly be said that the number of cheeses is only equalled by the number of those eating them, and space does not permit a full coverage of those available. The spectrum covers those from hard with a "bite" to the soft and creamy. Cheeses are in general made from cows' milk, but there are also those made from ewes' and goats' milk, indeed there are also speciality cheeses made from buffaloes' milk.

Fat content in cheeses is reckoned by the amount of fat contained in the dry matter (eg 60%) and the water content is not taken into account, so the apparent effect of this fat content is diminished according to the type of cheese, as summarised below.

<u>Hard cheeses</u> are those made with a hard or very hard paste and the longest of ripening and maturation times, which can vary between several months and years. The longer the ripening time the stronger the flavour and firmer the consistency. This category includes the hard cheeses, such as Parmesan and Provolone from Italy.

<u>Semi-hard Cheeses</u> are softer and moister than hard cheeses and their maturation times are less. The best-known of these are Cheddar from England, Comté and Beaufort from France, Emmental, Gruyère, Appenzell and Raclette from Switzerland, Pecorino from Italy, Bergkaäse, Tilsit and Wilstermarsch from Germany, Edam and Gouda from Holland, and Maribo and Havarti from Denmark.

Various semi-hard cheeses

*Bavarian Blue, Roquefort,
Gorgonzola, and Stilton*

<u>Semi-soft cheeses</u> exist in many varieties including butter-cream cheeses and blue cheeses. The best-known of the butter-cream cheeses are the Italian Bel Paese and the German Weisslacker and Steinbuscher, Port Salut and Reblochon from France, and Esrom from Denmark.
The best-known blue cheeses are Stilton from England, Gorgonzola from Italy, Bleu de Bresse and Roquefort (made from ewes' milk) from France, and Danish blue and Mycella from Denmark.
<u>Soft-Cheeses</u> differ from the semi-soft mainly by their higher water-content and include the white "flowered" cheeses such as Camembert and Brie and the orange-coloured cheeses with a stronger flavour, such as Münster from France, and Limburg and Romadur from Germany.
<u>Fresh Cheeses</u> cover all those which are not matured, made from either cream or milk, and include such names as quark, curd cheese and cream cheese, produced in many countries, Mozzarella and Robiola from Italy, Feta from Greece.
Most of the curd and cream cheeses are either sold as made, or can be further processed with the addition of fruit, vegetables or herbs.
<u>Sour milk cheeses</u> are also produced, mainly from allowing quark to sour, and is one of the oldest forms of cheese in the world. They exist with and without mould content. Many types are on sale, but in view of their character are not generally exported. Most have the distinctive sour milk flavour and a strong aroma.
<u>Processed cheeses</u> exist in many forms and can be made from most cheeses. The best-known are based on either cheddar or Emmental types.
Cheese should be stored in a cool place, preferably not in the refrigerator, wrapped in greaseproof (parchment) paper. Should it have been stored in a refrigerator, it should be taken out at least one hour before being required for use.

Assorted soft-cheeses

Handtools

Apple corer
Olive-shaped cutter
Small ball cutter
Ball (Pommes Parisienne) cutter
Asparagus peeler
Turning knife
Vegetable knife (Office knife)
Decorating knife (corrugated blade)
Saw-edged knife
Larding needle
Trussing needle
Egg slicer
Egg cutter (6 segment)
Radish cutter
Julienne cutter (zester)
Grooving knife
Boning knife
Cook's knife
Chopping knife
Pincers
Various pastry cutters (plain and corrugated)
Palette knife

Suitable Serving Dishes

STARTERS

Gravadlax with Leaf Salad and Prawn Salad

To serve 8:

1000 gr/2¼ lbs white asparagus

250 gr/9 oz peeled prawns

salt, pepper

juice of 1 lemon

1 frisée lettuce

1 lollo rosso or batavia lettuce

vinegar, oil

600 gr/21 oz sliced gravadlax (see p. 64)

green sauce (see p. 168)

Time Needed:

Preparation: 40 minutes
Service: 30 minutes

Advice

This starter can be easily prepared beforehand, provided that the dressing is not put on before service.

Preparation:

1. The asparagus is prepared as described on p. 127.
2. Dice the asparagus trimmings and mix with the prawns. Season with salt, pepper and lemon juice and put to one side.
3. Clean, wash and dry the salad leaves.
4. Prepare the dressing for the salad from oil, vinegar, salt and pepper.

Service:

5. Place the salad leaves at the top of the plate.
6. Arrange the asparagus tips in a fan shape at the bottom right corner of the plate, tips outwards, with the gravadlax in the bottom left corner with the prawns between.
7. Place a dessertspoonful of the sauce between the asparagus and gravadlax. Serve the remaining sauce separately.
8. Shortly before service, sprinkle the salad and asparagus tips with the dressing.

Salmon Tartare in Smoked Salmon Coating with Cress and Mustard Sauce

Preparation:

1. Chop the salmon fillet coarsely or pass through the coarse plate of a mincing machine. Season with lemon juice, salt and pepper.
2. Lay out the slices of smoked salmon onto a lightly oiled sheet of greaseproof (parchment) paper. Place the chopped salmon on top and roll up tightly. Place to cool in the refrigerator.
3. Clean and wash the various salad leaves and dry well. Dress with oil, vinegar, salt and pepper.

Service:

4. Dress the salad leaves onto the plate.
5. Cut the salmon roll diagonally into 16 slices, to allow 2 per portion.
6. Pour one spoonful of sauce between the salmon rolls and garnish with a little watercress. Serve the remaining sauce separately.

To serve 8:

400 gr/14 oz salmon fillet, completely boned
juice of 2 lemons
salt, pepper
400 gr/14 oz sliced smoked salmon
various salad leaves
vinegar, oil
cress and mustard sauce (see p. 169)
watercress to garnish

Time Needed:

Preparation time: 25 minutes (without cooling time)
Service time: 15 minutes

 Advice

Serve with French sticks or toasted white sandwich bread. The salmon roll used in this dish may be used as a garnish or component of a fish platter.

Terrine of Pike-Perch with Marinated Mange-Tout Peas

To serve 8:

400 gr/14 oz pike-perch fillet

6–7 egg whites (about 200 ml/7 fl. oz)

200 gr/7 oz cream

salt, pepper, nutmeg

a little Noilly Prat vermouth or white wine

100 gr/3½ oz salmon fillet

1 carrot

300 gr/11 oz mange-tout (sugar peas/snow peas)

1 radicchio lettuce

vinegar, oil

Tyrolean sauce (see p. 170)

Time Needed:

Prepare on the previous day
Pre-heat the oven to
150°C/275°F
Preparation time: 75 minutes
(without cooling time)
Service time: 20 minutes

 Advice

If the loaf tin is rinsed out with warm water before filling, the clingfilm will cling to the sides without creasing and ease the filling of the mould. The arrangement of carrot and salmon strips shown in the photograph may be changed as desired.

Preparation:

1. Skin the fillet of pike-perch from tail to head, then cut into small pieces.
2. Purée the fish in a food processor and add the egg whites and cream, beating until a creamy mass is made. Season with salt, pepper, a little Noilly Prat French vermouth and a little grated nutmeg.
3. Cut the salmon fillet lengthwise into 2 cm/¾″ strips.
4. Wash, peel and quarter the carrots lengthwise. Blanch briefly in boiling salted water, to remain crisp.
5. Line a 14 cm/6″ long loaf tin with oven-suitable clingfilm. Fill with part of the fish mixture and lay in alternate strips of salmon and carrot. Add some more fish mixture and repeat with the strips, finishing off with the remaining fish mixture.
6. Press the mixture down lightly with a spoon, and knock the base of the tin on the table top to remove any air bubbles.
7. Close the clingfilm over the top of the mixture, then wrap the whole tin in more clingfilm.
8. Poach the terrine in a water-bath in the oven at 150°C/275°F for about 30 minutes.
9. Remove the terrine from the water-bath and allow to cool in the tin. During cooling, place a weighted board on top of the terrine, if the filling is over the top, in order to ensure an even shape when sliced.
10. Prepare the mange-tout for the garnish. Cut half the quantity raw, into fine strips, and marinate with salt, pepper, vinegar and oil. Blanch the rest in boiling salted water leaving them crisp.
11. Clean, wash and dry the radicchio. Season with salt, pepper, vinegar and oil.

Service:

12. Turn out the terrine, remove the clingfilm and cut the terrine into slices.
13. Arrange the blanched mange-tout in a star shape on the plate, with pieces of the dressed radicchio leaves arranged between. In the centre of each plate place some Tyrolean sauce, with a slice of the terrine on top. Scatter the dressed strips of mange-tout around the outside.

The carrot strips are placed on the first layer of fish

Another layer of fish purée is placed on top

Finally a layer of purée is placed on the salmon strips

Mosaic of Salmon, Smoked Eel and Vegetables in Lettuce with Yoghurt and Chervil Sauce

To serve 8:

400 gr/14 oz green beet, chard or spinach leaves

100 gr/3½ oz fine Kenya green beans

2 carrots

180 gr/6 oz salmon fillet

salt, pepper

vinegar, oil

juice of 1 lemon

100 gr/3½ oz smoked eel fillet

200 gr/7 oz sliced smoked salmon

200 gr/7 oz fish aspic

Curly endive (Frisée) and radicchio for garnishing

Yoghurt and Chervil sauce (see p. 171)

Time Needed:

Prepare the previous day
Preparation: 60 minutes
(without cooling time)
Service: 20 minutes

Advice

This terrine can also be used to advantage as a garnish for various fish dishes.

Preparation:

1. Commence with the preparation of the vegetables for the terrine. Clean the beet leaves. Wash the leaves singly and remove the thick centre stalk. Blanch them quickly in salted water, then refresh in cold water before dabbing dry.
2. Clean the green beans and blanch them in salted water. Wash and peel the carrots, quarter them lengthwise and blanch them in salted water. Dry off the beans and carrots well.
3. Beat the salmon fillet flat and season it with salt, pepper and lemon juice. Roll it in clingfilm, tying the ends together. Poach it in salted water at 80°C/176°F for about 10 minutes, and allow to cool in the liquor.
4. Cut the smoked eel into three lengthwise.
5. Prepare to fill a 14 cm/5½″ terrine mould. It is best to cool it well, preferably in a freezer, then coat it evenly with a layer of fish aspic.
6. Line the mould with the blanched beet leaves allowing them to overhang the top edge.
7. Pass the smoked salmon slices quickly through the nearly cold fish aspic and lay these in the mould inside the beet leaves.
8. Lay half of the carrots, beans and smoked eel strips in the bottom of the mould and cover with some of the fish aspic.
9. Remove the salmon fillet from the clingfilm and place this in the centre of the mould adding some more aspic.
10. Now fill the mould with the remaining carrots, beans and strips of eel, as before and fill to the top with some more aspic.
11. Finally, close the mould first with the smoked salmon, then the beet leaves and fill to the brim with the remaining aspic. Allow to cool well.

Service:

12. Turn out the mould. Pass a knife blade around the edges of the mould. Pass the mould quickly under hot water, then turn out and allow to re-cool, afterwards cutting the terrine into eight even slices. An electric carving knife or one dipped into hot water will do this very well.
13. Clean the radicchio and frisée well, wash, dry and season with oil, vinegar, salt and pepper.
14. Garnish the upper part of the plate with the salad, laying the slice of terrine partly on the salad, and lastly pouring on the yoghurt and chervil sauce.

The smoked eel slices are laid in the mould

A layer of vegetables follows the salmon fillet

The mould is closed, first with the overhanging smoked salmon, then with the beet leaves

Crisp Salad Selection with Roast Duck Breast and Green Peppers

To serve 8:

4 dessertspoons raspberry vinegar

4 dessertspoons oil

salt, pepper

1 frisée lettuce

1 radicchio lettuce

1 batavia lettuce

1 oak-leaf lettuce

4 duck-breasts each of 200 gr/7 oz

100 ml/3½ fl. oz roast gravy (commercial product)

oil for frying

1 teaspoon green peppers

Time Necessary:

Preparation: 30 minutes
Service: 10 minutes

Preparation:

1. Make a dressing from raspberry vinegar, oil, salt and pepper.
2. Separate and clean the salad leaves, wash and dry well.
3. Remove some of the skin from the sides of the duck breasts and cut it in tiny dice.
4. Season the duck breasts with salt and pepper and fry them off in a pan with very little oil, skin sides first, then turn over and fry off lightly, then place in an oven heated to 200°C/400°F and cook for about 10 minutes. Put the diced skin into the pan with the duck breasts and cook off until crisp.
5. Take the duck breasts and dice from the pan and keep warm wrapped in aluminium foil.
6. Pour out the fat from the frying pan and deglaze the pan with some of the raspberry vinegar. Bring it to the boil and add the gravy. Let it cook out and keep it in a warm place.

Service:

7. Share the salad between the plates, and dress it with the raspberry vinegar dressing.
8. Cut the duck breasts lengthwise into strips and arrange into a star shape on top of the salad leaves. Sprinkle with the roasting liquor, and finally scatter the duck skin dice and green peppercorns. The duck breast should be served lukewarm.

Part of the duck-skin is removed

Mould of Rabbit with Carrots, Green Beans, and Mushroom Salad

To serve 8:

1 rabbit (about 1500 gr/3¼ lbs)

1 onion

80 gr/3 oz carrots

80 gr/3 oz celery

80 gr/3 oz leeks

15 sheets gelatine (check against packet instructions!)

4 carrots

200 gr/7 oz green kenya beans

4 beef tomatoes

oil for frying

250 gr/9 oz fresh mushrooms

1 batavia lettuce or other crisp salad leaves

juice of 1 lemon

salt, pepper

vinegar, oil

Time Necessary:

Preparation on the previous day
Preparation: 1 hr 10 min
(without cooling time)
Service: 10 minutes

Preparation:

1. Turn the rabbit on to its back. Remove the hind legs and the fore legs, using a sharp knife, then joint each leg.
2. Remove the fillets along the back by boning out from the back bone, and remove any skin.
3. Remove liver and kidneys from the rib-cage.
4. Remove any sinews from the leg joints, remove skin and bone. The flesh from the hind legs, fillets, liver and kidneys can be used to make the jelly. The fore legs and belly parts can be used to make a ragout separately, or put to freeze.
5. Cut up the carcase, leg bones and trimmings and fry them off well in a little oil.
6. Peel the onion and root vegetables, cut up small, then fry off with the bones etc., then wet with 1½ litres/2¾ pints water.
7. Bring the stock to the boil and cook off for about 30 minutes.
8. Finally strain through a cloth then reduce the stock to 1 litre.
9. Soften the gelatine in cold water, drain off and beat in to the hot stock. Season the stock with some salt.
10. While the stock is cooking, prepare the vegetables. Wash and peel the carrots and quarter them lengthwise, then blanch in boiling salted water leaving them crisp.
11. Clean the green beans and blanch if necessary in salted water.
12. Remove the stalks and cores from the beef tomatoes and blanch the fruit. Remove the skins, cut into quarters and remove the seeds.
13. The meat is now prepared. Season the legs, fillets, liver and kidneys with salt and pepper, and fry off in some oil for about 10 minutes, keeping the flesh pink. Allow to cool thoroughly.
14. Line a 14 cm/5″ loaf tin with a suitable clingfilm. Pour in some of the stock and allow to set. Place the carrots and beans in as layers.
15. Pour in another layer of stock and allow almost to set.
16. As a middle layer, between the vegetable strips lay in the meat and lay in the liver and kidneys, if used. Then fill with more stock.
17. Now follows a layer of carrots and beans, finishing with the tomatoes and the remaining stock.
18. Put the mould into the refrigerator to cool thoroughly.

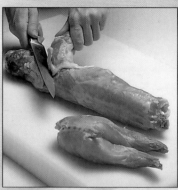

Remove the hind- and fore-legs at the joints

Bone the fillets

The fried-off meat as the middle layer in the mould

Finally, the tomato is placed in the mould

Service:

19. Clean and wash the mushrooms and cut into slices.
20. Clean, wash and dry the salad leaves.
21. Alternate salad and mushroom slices around the edge of the plate.
22. Turn out the mould, and using a warmed knife cut it into 8 even slices. Place a slice in the centre of the plate.
23. Make a dressing from the lemon juice, vinegar, oil, salt and pepper and sprinkle over both the salad leaves and mould.

Parma Ham with Sweet and Sour Pickled Vegetables

To serve 8:

1 carrot

1 courgette (zucchini)

8 young leeks

½ cauliflower

2 heads broccoli (240 gr/8 oz)

1 green capsicum

50 gr/1¾ oz sugar

100 ml/3½ fl. oz wine vinegar

500 gr/18 oz Parma ham (sliced)

various salad leaves for garnishing

salt, pepper

vinegar, oil

Time Necessary:

Prepare vegetables the previous day
Preparation: 30 minutes
Leave vegetables in stock for 24 hours
Service: 10 minutes

Preparation:

1. Peel the carrots and cut into 5 mm/¼" thick slices, using a corrugated decorating knife.
2. Wash the courgette (zucchini) and peel it so that some strips of peel are left showing.
3. Remove the roots from the young leeks and cut off the tops just where the colour changes to green. Wash thoroughly, without cutting the stalk.
4. Put the broccoli and cauliflower briefly into salted water, then break into florets and wash thoroughly.
5. Clean and remove the seeds from the capsicum, then cut it into 8 lengthwise. Wash thoroughly then cut into diamond shapes.
6. Heat the sugar in a pan until it caramelises. Deglaze with the vinegar and add some water. Bring to the boil.
7. Put the vegetables into the stock individually in the following order, and allow to cook for about half a minute. Carrots, cauliflower, capsicum, leek, courgette (zucchini), and broccoli.
8. Allow the vegetables to get cold in the stock for 24 hours.

Service:

9. Fold the Parma ham lengthwise and arrange it into a semi circle on the left side of the plate with the slices overlapping one another a little.
10. Clean the salad leaves, wash them, season them with salt, pepper, oil and vinegar and lay them on the right-hand side of the plate. Lay the sweet-sour vegetables on to the salad leaves.

The carrot is first peeled, then cut with a decorating knife into slices

The courgette is peeled so that some strips of peel are left on it

Vegetable Royal with Chive Cream Cheese and Smoked Pork Loin

To serve 8:

200 gr/7 oz green Kenya beans

2 large carrots

2 medium-sized courgettes (zucchini)

2 heads broccoli 240 gr/8 oz

¼ cauliflower

4 eggs

100 gr/3½ oz cream

salt, pepper, nutmeg

300 gr/12¼ oz chive cream cheese (see p. 171)

250 gr/9 oz smoked pork loin or rolled smoked pork loin (lachsschinken)

Time Necessary:

Prepare the day before
Preparation: 1 hr 40 min (without cooling time)
Service: 20 minutes

 Advice

This vegetable terrine, if cut into half-slices, may also be used as a garnish to a roast meat dish.

Preparation:

1. Clean the green beans, removing strings if necessary. Blanch them in salted water leaving them crisp, then refresh immediately and drain off until dry.
2. Wash the carrots, peel them and according to size, cut them either into quarters or sixths. Blanch them briefly then refresh and drain off until dry.
3. Wash and quarter the courgettes.
4. Wash and clean the broccoli and cauliflower in salted water, cut into florets, then blanch quickly in salted water. Refresh and drain off.
5. Whisk the eggs with the cream and season well with salt, pepper and nutmeg.
6. Line a loaf tin with clingfilm. Put in a little of the egg mixture and arrange the vegetables on top in layers. Pour over the remaining egg mixture.
7. Cover the loaf tin with clingfilm and put it into a water bath in the oven set at about 120°C/240°F and allow to cook (poach) for about 60 minutes. Check the temperature using a meat thermometer and do not allow it to go above 70°C/158°F.
8. Take the vegetable terrine from the oven and allow to cool in the loaf tin.

Service:

9. Turn out the terrine from the loaf tin, remove the clingfilm and cut it into 8 even-sized slices.
10. Lay out the slices on to the top half of a serving dish. Shape the slices of smoked pork loin into roses. Place three roses vertically under each slice of terrine. Place a heap of the chive cream cheese to left and right of the dish.

Carpaccio of Marinated Beef Fillet with Green Asparagus Tips

To serve 8:

500 gr/18 oz fillet (cut from centre) or eye of sirloin

1 bunch chives

1 bunch parsley

100 ml/3½ fl. oz olive oil

juice of 2 lemons

salt, black pepper

1000 gr/2¼ lbs green asparagus

1 Belgian endive (chicory)

1 radicchio

vinegar, oil

salt, pepper

Time Necessary:

Preparation: 30 minutes
Service: 15 minutes
Marinade: 15 minutes

 Advice

In the asparagus season, white asparagus may be substituted for the green variety.

Preparation:

1. Remove any sinews and skin from the meat and place it in the freezer for 15 minutes to firm up in order that it may be sliced thinly.
2. Wash the chives and parsley well and cut up finely, or chop very small.
3. Mix the olive oil with the lemon juice, and add the finely chopped herbs. Season with salt and pepper.
4. Prepare and cook the green asparagus, as described on p. 127.
5. Finally, clean, wash and dry the radicchio and endive.
6. Make a dressing from oil, vinegar, salt and pepper.

Service:

7. Using a brush, paint some of the dressing onto the lower part of the plate.
8. Cut the frosted beef fillet into paper-thin slices and arrange them fanwise on to the dressing coated part of the plate.
9. Coat the sliced meat with the rest of the dressing and allow to stand for at least 15 minutes.
10. Arrange two slices of endive parallel to each other at the top part of the plate in the centre.
11. Arrange the asparagus, tips outwards, onto the slices of beef.
12. Place the radicchio between the endive leaves and the asparagus. Sprinkle with the salad dressing.

Courgettes (Zucchini) and Tomato Quiche with Cress Purée

To serve 8:

350 gr/12 oz Puff-pastry
3 tomatoes
2 courgettes (zucchini)
2 eggs
120 gr/4 fl. oz cream
salt, pepper
thyme, oregano
600 ml/21 fl. oz cress purée (see p. 172)
watercress for garnish

600 ml/21 fl. oz cress purée (see p. 172)

Time Necessary:

Pre-heat the oven to
200°C/400°F
Preparation: 35 minutes
Service: 10 minutes

Preparation:

1. Roll out the puff-pastry to 5 mm/¼″ thickness and line a 28 cm/11″ loose-bottomed quiche pan or springform mould with it.
2. Wash the tomatoes, remove the centre core and cut the fruit into slices.
3. Wash and clean the courgettes (zucchini) and cut them into slices.
4. Lay the slices of tomato and courgette alternately in the pastry case to cover the bottom.
5. Beat the eggs and cream together and season with salt and pepper. Pour the custard mixture carefully into the pastry case, over the vegetables. Sprinkle all over with a little thyme and oregano.
6. Cook the quiche on the middle shelf of the oven, heated to 200°C/400°F, for about 20 minutes, then take out and allow to cool.

Service:

7. Put a small circle of the cress purée on each plate.
8. Cut the quiche into 8 even portions.
9. Place 1 portion of quiche on to the cress purée and garnish with a small sprig of watercress.

A Selection of Canapés

These small titbits can be equally used as hors d'oeuvre
with aperitifs or for a reception. Smoked salmon with
salmon caviar, Parma ham with green asparagus, or duck
breast with segments of orange and pistachio nuts are only
a selection of the ideas which can be used to make these
refined delicacies. They cater for all tastes and prepare the
palate for further treats to come.

Production of Canapés:

In most cases canapés are made using white bread as a base, but pumpernickel or wholemeal bread may also be used according to taste. The bread is buttered, but mayonnaise (see p. 168) may be used instead, which will produce a moister canapé. The slices of white bread may be cut either into squares or triangles or into circles, using a pastry cutter. When cut out, the bread may be laid onto a dampened kitchen cloth in order to reduce drying-out.

Smoked Salmon with Salmon Caviar

Preparation:

1. Wash and dry the radicchio leaves, and lay them on to the slices of bread.
2. Form the smoked salmon into rosettes and lay them on top.
3. Pipe some horseradish cream on top.
4. Garnish with the salmon caviar and a sprig of chervil.

For 6 Canapés:

6 leaves of radicchio

6 circles of buttered white bread

6 slices of smoked salmon

3 dessertspoonsful of horseradish cream (see p. 172)

60 gr/2 oz Salmon caviar

6 sprigs chervil

Time Necessary:

Preparation: 10 minutes

Parma Ham with Green Asparagus

Preparation:

1. If using fresh asparagus, cut the tips into 4 cm/1½ in lengths and cook for 5 to 7 minutes in salted water. Refresh in cold water and dry off well.
2. Wash the radicchio leaves well, dry and lay them on to the bread circles.
3. Cover with the Parma ham, and garnish with two asparagus tips.

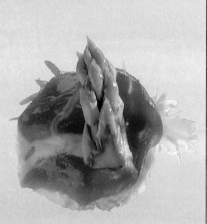

For 6 Canapés:

12 sticks green asparagus (fresh or canned)

leaves of radicchio

6 circles of buttered white bread

6 slices of Parma ham (each of 15 gr/½ oz)

Time Necessary:

Preparation: 15 minutes

Matjes Herring Tartare with Apple

For 6 Canapés:

1 apple

juice of 1 lemon

6 circles of buttered white bread

150 gr/5¼ oz Matjes herring fillets

1 bunch chives

Time Necessary:

Preparation: 10 minutes

Preparation:

1. Peel the apple and cut into 6 slices each 5 mm/¼ in thick. Sprinkle them with lemon juice and lay them on to the prepared white bread circles. Cut the remaining apple into tiny cubes.
2. Soak the Matjes herring fillets if necessary, dry them and cut them into tiny cubes. Mix with the apple cubes and sprinkle them with lemon juice.
3. Place the Matjes salad on the apple slices.
4. Wash the chives, dry, chop finely and place a sprinkle on top of the canapés.

Prawns with Quails' Eggs

For 6 Canapés:

1 salad cucumber

6 buttered circles of white bread

120 gr/4 oz peeled prawns

juice of 1 lemon

3 dessertspoons yoghurt

1 teaspoon chopped dill-weed

salt, pepper

3 quails' eggs (bottled)

6 sprigs dill-weed

Time Necessary:

Preparation: 10 minutes

Preparation:

1. Wash the cucumber. Peel the cucumber using a zesting-knife so as to leave strips of peel on the cucumber. Cut off sufficient slices of cucumber and lay them on the circles of bread.
2. Marinate the prawns in the lemon juice then divide them between the prepared slices of bread.
3. Mix the chopped dill-weed with the yoghurt, beating well, then seasoning with the salt and pepper. Napp (coat) the prawns with the sauce.
4. Place a halved quail's egg on top and garnish with a sprig of dill-weed.

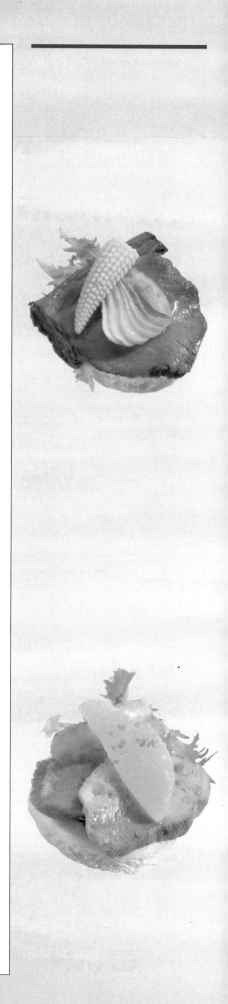

Roast Beef with Miniature Corn-Cobs and Gherkins

For 6 Canapés:

6 slices of buttered white bread cut into circles

some frisée lettuce

6 slices underdone roast beef

6 small pickled gherkins (dill pickles)

3 miniature corn-cobs

Time Necessary:

Preparation: 5 minutes

Preparation:

1. Cover the prepared slice of bread with a piece of frisée lettuce.
2. Lay a slice of roast beef on top.
3. Using a sharp pointed knife, slice the gherkin thinly, but only to three-quarters of its length, then press it out, fanwise. Halve the corn-cob lengthwise.
4. Decorate the canapés with the gherkin fan and corn-cob.

Duck Breast with Orange Segments and Pistachio Nuts

For 6 Canapés:

1 boned duck breast (250 gr/9 oz)

salt and pepper

1 dessertspoon oil

6 slices buttered white bread cut into circles

some frisée lettuce

1 orange

1 teaspoon chopped pistachio nuts

Time Necessary:

Pre-heat the oven to 200°C/400°F
Preparation: 25 minutes

Preparation:

1. Trim the duck breast free from fat and sinews. Season with salt and pepper. Fry off in oil and while the oven is being used for other items, cook off for about 10 minutes at 200°C/400°F.
2. While cooking, cover the prepared slices of bread with the frisée lettuce.
3. Peel the oranges to the flesh and cut into segments.
4. Slice the cooled duck breast into 12 slices allowing 2 slices for each canapé.
5. Garnish with the orange segments and sprinkle with the chopped pistachio nuts.

Tomatoes with Cream Cheese and Chives

For 6 Canapés:

3 small tomatoes

150 gr/5 oz cream cheese
(quark)

3 dessertspoons cream or milk

salt and pepper

1 bunch chives

6 stuffed olives

cocktail sticks or tooth picks

6 slices buttered white bread cut
into circles

Time Necessary:

Preparation: 15 minutes

Preparation:

1. Wash the tomatoes, remove the core, and blanch for about 5 to 8 seconds in boiling water, then refresh immediately in cold water. Remove the skins, then halve crosswise. Remove the seeds and cut each half to the same height.
2. Mix the cream cheese (quark) with cream or milk to a smooth paste, then season with salt and pepper.
3. Wash the chives, then cut or chop finely and add to the cheese mixture. Fill into the tomato halves.
4. Stick the olives onto the cocktail sticks. Place the tomato halves on the bread circles, and hold firm with the cocktail sticks.

Camembert Cream with Grapes

For 6 Canapés:

100 gr/3½ oz Camembert

50 gr/1¾ oz butter

1 teaspoon paprika

salt, pepper

some radicchio leaves

6 slices buttered white bread cut
into circles

a few grapes

6 crackers

Time Necessary:

Preparation: 15 minutes

Preparation:

1. Mix the Camembert with the butter and beat until smooth. Season with salt, pepper and paprika.
2. Place a piece of radicchio on to each circle of bread and pipe out a rosette of the cheese mixture in the centre.
3. Garnish with the grape and cracker.

Salmon Medallions with Prawns and Stuffed Olives

To serve 6:

200 gr/7 oz salmon fillet (boned)

juice of 1 lemon

salt, pepper

1 hard-boiled egg

20 gr/¾ oz butter

1 teaspoon mustard

6 peeled prawns

6 stuffed olives

Time Necessary:

Preparation: 35 minutes (without cooling)

Preparation:

1. Beat out the salmon fillet lightly. Season with lemon juice, salt and pepper.
2. Roll the salmon fillet in suitable clingfilm and fasten the ends. Poach the rolled salmon fillet in a water bath for about 15 minutes at about 70°C/158°F.
3. Allow the salmon to cool in the water bath.
4. Shell the egg and pass the yolk through a hair sieve. Mix it with butter and mustard to a smooth paste and season with salt and pepper.
5. Unwrap the salmon fillet from the clingfilm, dab it dry and finally cut it with a sharp knife into 6 equal medallions.
6. Pipe some of the egg paste on top of each medallion. Place a prawn on top of each.
7. Halve the olives and garnish the medallions with one half.

Bouchées Filled with Roquefort Cream

To serve 6:

80 gr/3 oz Roquefort cheese

60 gr/2 oz butter

2 radishes

6 small puff-pastry vol-au-vent cases

Time Necessary:

Preparation: 20 minutes

Preparation:

1. Pass the Roquefort cheese and butter through a hair sieve, then beat until smooth.
2. Wash the radishes and cut off the ends. Halve the radishes and cut into 12 slices.
3. Put the Roquefort cream into a piping bag with a star tube and fill the bouchées.
4. Garnish each with 2 slices of radish.

 Advice

Small vol-au-vent cases may be purchased ready-made if desired.

Pork Fillet with Liver Mousse and Walnuts

To serve 6:

| 200 gr/7 oz pork fillet |
| salt, pepper |
| 2 dessertspoons oil |
| 50 gr/1¾ oz calves' liver sausage |
| 40 gr/1½ oz butter |
| 10 ml/⅓ fl. oz port |
| 6 walnut kernels |
| 6 mandarin or orange segments |

Time Necessary:

Pre-heat the oven to
180°C/350°F
Preparation: 25 minutes
(without cooling)

Preparation:

1. Season the pork fillet with salt and pepper and tie into shape with kitchen twine.
2. Heat the oil into a frying pan and fry off the fillet all over. Place it in an oven pre-heated to 180°C/350°F with other items and roast for about 8 minutes so that it is still pink. Check by thumb pressure whether it is cooked. If the meat still gives under pressure then it is just right.
3. Take the fillet immediately from the pan and let it cool thoroughly.
4. Pass the calves' liver sausage through a hair sieve with the butter, mixing it well together, and season with the port.
5. Cut the pork fillet into 6 even-sized medallions.
6. Pipe out the liver mousse onto the pork fillet medallions and garnish with the walnut kernels and orange or mandarin segments.

Salmon Tartare on Pumpernickel with Quail's Egg and Chervil

To serve 6:

| 200 gr/7 oz salmon fillet |
| juice of 1 lemon |
| salt, pepper |
| 6 slices cucumber |
| 6 small rounds pumpernickel |
| 3 quail's eggs (bottled) |
| 1 sprig of chervil |

Time Necessary:

Preparation: 20 minutes

Preparation:

1. Chop the salmon fillet finely. Season it with lemon juice, salt and pepper.
2. Trim the cucumber slices to the same size as the pumpernickel rounds and lay them on top.
3. Form 6 equal sized balls of the salmon tartare with a spoon and place one on each slice of cucumber.
4. Halve the quail's eggs lengthwise and press one half on each ball of salmon.
5. Garnish each quail's egg with a leaf of chervil.

Croustades with Cherry Tomatoes and White Fish Caviar

To serve 6:

6 cherry tomatoes

60 gr/2 oz whitefish caviar

40 gr/1½ oz soured cream (crème fraîche)

salt, pepper

some frisée lettuce

6 croustades (commercial product)

Time Necessary:

Preparation: 15 minutes

 Advice

Commercially produced croustades can be purchased from delicatessen suppliers, or can be made from circles of puff-pastry.

Preparation:

1. Wash the cherry tomatoes, remove the cores and cut off the top at three-quarters of the height to form a lid.
2. Remove the seeds and some of the flesh, using a teaspoon handle.
3. Beat the caviar with the soured cream (crème fraîche) and season with salt and pepper.
4. Fill the cream into the tomatoes.
5. Clean the frisée lettuce and dry well.
6. Tear the salad leaves into small pieces, lay them onto the croustades, and place the tomatoes on top.

Stuffed Mushrooms with Green Asparagus and Truffle

To serve 6:

6 green asparagus tips

6 large mushroom heads (caps)

juice of 1 lemon

50 gr/1¾ oz fine calves' liver sausage

40 gr/1½ oz butter

10 ml/⅓ fl. oz port

1 small truffle

Time Necessary:

Preparation: 30 minutes

Preparation:

1. Halve the asparagus tips in the middle and blanch them in salted water.
2. Remove the stalks from the mushroom heads, wash the heads and blanch them briefly in lemon water.
3. Dry the asparagus and mushroom heads thoroughly.
4. Beat the calves' liver sausage with the butter and flavour with the port.
5. Lay the mushroom heads on the work surface with the open side uppermost. Cut the asparagus tips across diagonally and place on the mushroom head with the tip pointing outwards.
6. Pipe the liver mousse into the mushroom heads, using a star tube.
7. Cut the truffle into 6 slices, and from each cut two ovals, using an oval cutter.
8. Garnish each mushroom head with two ovals of truffle.

Roast Beef Rolls with Tomatoes and Eggs

To serve 6:

1 tomato

1 hard-boiled egg

3 pickled gherkins (small dill pickles)

6 slices underdone roast beef

Time Necessary:

Preparation: 10 minutes

Preparation:

1. Blanch the tomato in boiling water, refresh in cold water, and remove the skin. Cut the tomato in half, remove the seeds, and cut each half into three.
2. Shell the hard-boiled egg and cut into six. Finally cut the gherkins in halves lengthwise.
3. Lay out the roast beef slices individually. Lay on each slice a piece of tomato, a segment of egg and a half of gherkin. Roll up the short side of the roast beef slices.
4. Cut the ends square. Cut the rolls two-thirds deep in the centre, and bend the ends downwards, so that the cut side shows uppermost.

Artichoke Bottoms with Vegetables

To serve 6:

1 carrot

1 white turnip

120 gr/4 oz broccoli

2 dessertspoons vinegar

1 dessertspoon oil

salt, pepper

some water

6 artichoke bottoms (canned)

Time Necessary:

Preparation: 30 minutes

Preparation:

1. Wash the carrot and turnip. Cut each into six and turn each piece.
2. Wash the broccoli and break it into 6 equal parts.
3. Bring a pan to the boil containing oil, vinegar, salt and pepper and some water. Put in the vegetables and cook till just firm (al dente). Allow to cool thoroughly.
4. Cut the artichoke bottom flat so that it will stand. Drain the vegetables well and arrange them onto the artichoke bottom.

FISH
AND SHELLFISH

Country-Style Fish Dish with Various Horseradish Sauces

To serve 8:

4 peppered, smoked mackerel fillets

4 smoked rollmops

8 to 12 slices smoked halibut

250 gr/8 oz Schillerlocken (smoked rock-salmon fillet strips)

2 untreated lemons

various salad leaves

green and black olives

horseradish cream (see p. 172)

cranberry and horseradish sauce (see p. 172)

Time Necessary:

Preparation: 20 minutes
Service: 15 minutes

Preparation:

1. Remove the skin from the smoked mackerel fillets, and cut them across diagonally. If very large, cut them into three.
2. Remove the skewers from the rollmops but leave them rolled and cut each into half to produce thin rolls.
3. Cut the schillerlocken (smoked rock-salmon fillets) diagonally into 5 cm/2" lengths.
4. Wash the lemon and groove all round with a grooving-knife. Halve the lemon lengthwise and cut each half into slices. Cut the second lemon in two Vandyke style (with points).

Service:

5. Arrange the smoked fish on an oval dish, the mackerel fillets overlapping, following the line of the dish on one side with the rollmop slices arranged inside them.
6. The slices of halibut are laid overlapping each other on the opposite side of the dish, fanwise, and decorated with the grooved lemon slices.

7. The central area of the dish is decorated with the various salad leaves around the outside, and in the central area the schillerlocken, pointing outwards and the olives in the centre. Finally, the lemon halves are placed at each end of the dish. The horseradish sauces are served in sauceboats, separately.

Prime Smoked Fish Dish with Prawns and Avocados, Horseradish Cream and Mustard and Dill Sauce

The smoked eel is cut from head to tail in diagonal slices

To serve 8:

250 gr/9 oz smoked salmon
250 gr/9 oz smoked eel
8 fillets smoked trout
160 gr/6 oz peeled prawns
1 ripe avocado
juice of 2 lemons
salt, pepper
curly endive (frisée), oak-leaf lettuce, few leaves of radicchio and sprigs of dill-weed
Horseradish cream (see p. 172)
Mustard and dill sauce (see p. 170)

Time Necessary:

Preparation: 40 minutes
Service: 20 minutes

Preparation:

1. Prepare the smoked fish. Remove any remaining fine bones with pliers or tweezers from head to tail. Cut into thin slices in the opposite direction.
2. Prepare the smoked eel. First remove the centre bone from head to tail.
3. Now remove the skin from each half of the fish and cut across diagonally into slices.
4. Remove the skin from the trout. Cut across at the head-end at an angle, then cut the fillet into two diagonally.
5. Marinate the prawns in a little lemon juice seasoned with salt and pepper.
6. Halve the avocado lengthwise and split into two, then remove the stone. Remove the flesh whole from the skin, using a dessertspoon.
7. Cut each half into even-sized segments and immediately srinkle them with the remaining lemon juice to prevent them going brown.

Service:

8. Arrange the smoked fish in an arc on a dish, with the smoked trout fillets at the top, overlapping.
   Under these place the smoked eel slices following the same curve.
9. Place the smoked salmon slices in a curve at the bottom part of the dish.

10. Decorate the central area of the dish with the salad leaves, the prawns in the centre on top. Garnish with the sprigs of dill-weed.
11. Place the segments of avocado into the upper corners of the dish.
12. Serve the sauces for this fish dish separately.

Preparation of Gravadlax

To serve 8:

1 leek
3 carrots
½ celeriac (about 300 gr/11 oz)
2 bunches parsley
1 bunch samphire
1 bunch borage
1 bunch salad burnet
1 bunch chervil
2 bunches chives
2 bunches dill-weed
300 gr/11 oz salt
200 gr/7 oz sugar
1 bayleaf
6–8 juniper berries
1 salmon (about 2000 gr/4½ lbs)
a few sprigs dill-weed as garnish

Time Necessary:

Prepare 2 days before needed
Preparation: 30 minutes
Marination: 1 day
Service: 20 minutes

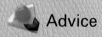 Advice

The salmon marinade can be used more than once. If the fish is allowed to stand for a day after marination it will become firmer and much easier to slice.

Preparation:

1. Wash the vegetables and herbs thoroughly.
2. Chop the parsley, samphire, borage, salad burnet, and chervil finely. Cut up finely the chives and dill-weed.
3. Peel the carrots and celeriac and cut into fine dice.
4. Halve the leek lengthwise, washing again, if necessary, then cut across into fine strips.
5. For the marinade mix the sugar and salt together with the prepared herbs and vegetables, a bayleaf and the juniper berries.
6. Scale the salmon from tail to head. Remove the head from just behind the gills. Free the fillets from the backbone.
7. Leave both fillets in the marinade for about 12 hours.
8. Take the salmon from the marinade, removing any remaining marinade from the fish. Remove any bones from the belly cavity using a sharp knife, working in a downward direction.
9. Should any fine bones be visible on the flesh side of the fillets, these should be removed, using a pair of tweezers, or fine pliers.

Service:

10. Slice the salmon fillets very thinly from tail to head and arrange on the service-dish. Garnish with a few sprigs of dill-weed.

The head is removed behind the gills

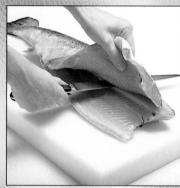

The fillets are removed along the backbone

The bones in the belly cavity are removed after marination

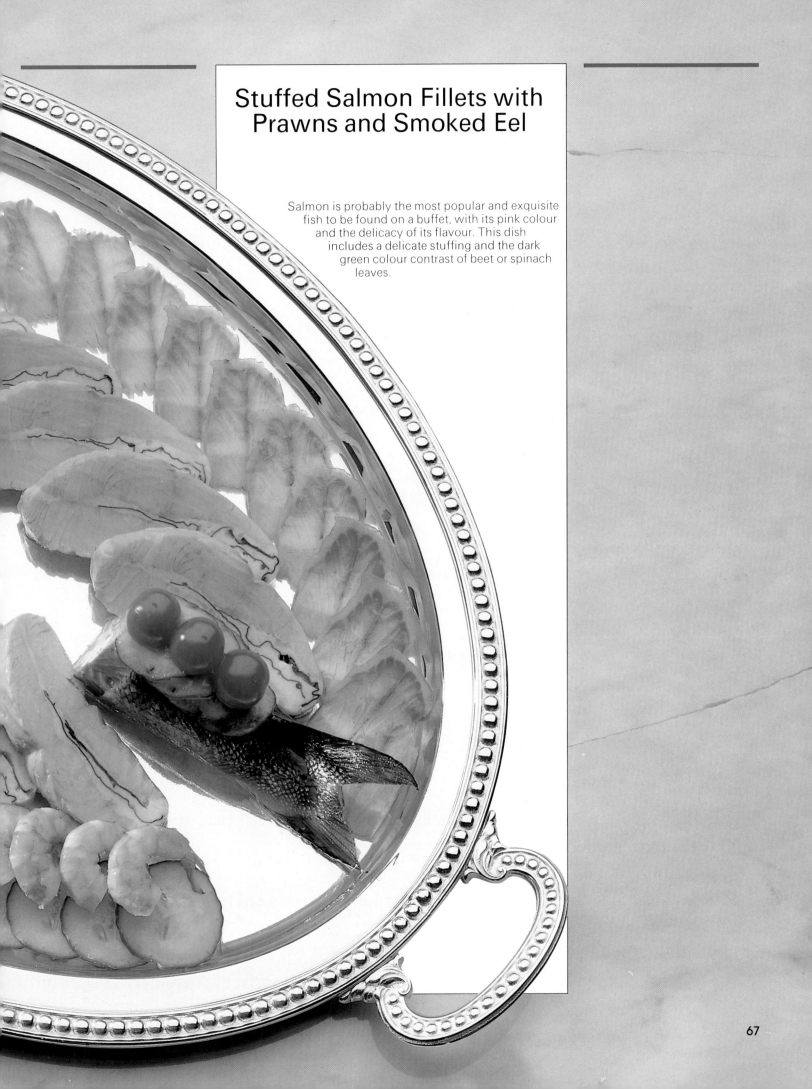

Stuffed Salmon Fillets with Prawns and Smoked Eel

Salmon is probably the most popular and exquisite fish to be found on a buffet, with its pink colour and the delicacy of its flavour. This dish includes a delicate stuffing and the dark green colour contrast of beet or spinach leaves.

Stuffed Salmon Fillets with Prawns and Smoked Eel

To serve 8:

1 salmon (about 2000 gr/4½ lbs)
150 gr/5¼ oz pike-perch fillet
150 gr/5¼ fl. oz cream
1 egg white
1 cl/⅓ fl. oz Pernod
salt, pepper
400 gr/14 oz beet or spinach leaves
juice of 1 lemon
2 litres/70 fl. oz Court-bouillin (see p. 75)
16 fresh prawns
250 gr/9 oz smoked eel
6 cherry tomatoes
1 small salad cucumber
100 gr/3½ oz fish aspic

Time Necessary:

Preparation: 70 minutes
(without cooling)
Service: 60 minutes

Advice

Cover the rear side of the salmon head with overlapping slices of cucumber.
Fill the eye cavities with butter and decorate with slices of olive.

Preparation:

1. Scale the salmon from tail to head, using the back of a knife.
2. Cut off the head with a sloping cut, about 3 cm/1¼″ behind the gills.
3. Cut off the tail level with the fleshy fin.
4. Place the head and tail into a clean kitchen cloth, and tie up for later attention.
5. Free both fillets from the backbone with a knife.
6. Cut out the bones from the inner side of the belly cavity, using a sharp knife.
7. Now skin the fillets. Begin at the tail end and cut off the skin towards the head, using a light pressure.
8. With tweezers or a pair of small pliers, remove any bones from the inner side of the salmon fillets.
9. For the stuffing, cut up the pike-perch fillets very small, or pass them through a food processor or a blender. Add the cream and egg white little by little. Season with the Pernod, salt and pepper.
10. Remove the stalks from the beet or spinach leaves. Wash well, then blanch for a moment in boiling salted water, refresh in cold water, then drain well.
11. Season the salmon fillets with salt and pepper.
12. Place one fillet, skin side down, on a sheet of suitable clingfilm.
13. Spread the fillet with one-third of the stuffing, with less at the outside edges.
14. Now lay the beet or spinach leaves out on top of the stuffing, spreading some more of the stuffing on top. Repeat the last two processes.
15. Now lay the second fillet on top of the first, skin-side uppermost. Press both fillets together lightly to re-form the shape of the fish, and wrap the whole up in the clingfilm, tying the ends of the package with twine.
16. Place the stuffed salmon fillets together with the cloth containing the head and tail into the cold court-bouillon, and heat to 95°C/203°F.
17. When the temperature is reached, throw in the prawns, take the pan from the stove, leaving the fish and prawns to poach in the liquor, and allow to cool, also in the liquor.
18. Remove the backbone from the smoked eel, then remove the skin.
19. Cut both eel fillets into slices.
20. Remove the salmon from the clingfilm. Peel the prawns and halve them lengthwise.

The bones from the inner side of the fillet are removed

Remaining bones from the inner side of the fillets are removed with tweezers

The salmon fillet is spread with the stuffing

A layer of beet leaves takes care of the delicate marbling of the light coloured filling

The dark layer of fat is carefully removed with a knife

The head and tail are cut level at the bottom so that they will stand on the dish

Service:

21. The upper and lower surfaces of the stuffed salmon are freed from any fat, then the fish is cut into neat, even slices.
22. The fish head and tail are cut at the bottom, to provide a flat, level surface to be placed on the serving dish. Remove the skin from the cut area and remove any underlying fat from beneath the skin.
23. Wash the cucumber and cut it into thin slices.
24. According to size, lay 4 to 5 slices of cucumber on the head and tail, and garnish with the cherry tomatoes. Fix these on, if necessary with some fish aspic.
25. Lay the head and the tail at each end of an oval serving dish. Arrange the salmon slices in two parallel lines curving slightly outwards, between head and tail.

26. On the upper curve of the dish arrange the slices of smoked eel overlapping each other.
27. On the lower curve of the dish arrange a row of cucumber slices, and garnish them with the prawn halves.

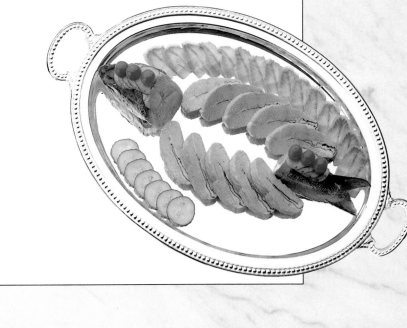

Stuffed Pike-Perch with Vegetable Salad in Artichoke Bottoms

To serve 8:

1 pike-perch (un-dressed weight about 1500 gr/3¼ lbs)

2 carrots

1 small onion

1 leek

1 untreated lemon

300 ml/10½ fl. oz vinegar

1 bayleaf

salt, pepper

400 gr/14 oz beet leaves or spinach

150 gr/5¼ oz fillet of salmon

about 100 gr/3½ fl. oz cream

2 egg whites

10 ml/⅓ fl. oz Pernod

6 pieces each turned carrot and courgette (zucchini)

some fish aspic

8 slices smoked salmon

8 artichoke bottoms with vegetables (see p. 57)

yoghurt and chervil sauce (see p. 171)

Time Necessary:

Preparation: 1 hr 50 min (without cooling time)
Service: 10 minutes

 Advice

It is best to cook pike-perch the day before it is needed, and allow it to cool overnight. The colder it is the easier it will be to slice.

Preparation:

1. Scale the pike-perch with the back of a knife from tail to head, before gutting.
2. Beginning at the dorsal fin, cut open the back and remove the back bone. Cut through the bone behind the head and at the front of the tail with scissors.
3. Cut further down without cutting the belly skin, in order to gain access to the intestines and remove them.
4. Discard the intestines, and retaining the bones removed, wash the prepared fish thoroughly and allow to drain.
5. Prepare the stock in which to poach the fish. Wash the vegetables, and cut up small. Wash and halve the lemon.
6. Place the ingredients, together with the vinegar, bayleaf, salt, pepper and fishbones in a wide flat pan together with about 5 litres/9 pints (U.K.)/ 11 pints (U.S.) of water, and bring to the boil.
7. In between times, prepare the filling. Remove the stalks from the beet or spinach leaves, then wash the leaves thoroughly in water before blanching them quickly in boiling salted water. Refresh in cold water and allow to drain well.
8. For the stuffing, cut up the salmon fillets very small, or pass them through a food processor or a blender, working the mixture well, until a smooth paste results. Season with the Pernod, salt and pepper.
9. Lay out the beet or spinach leaves the length of the cavity in the fish and spread on them about one-half of the stuffing. Roll up the leaves into a cigar shape.
10. Season the inside surfaces of the gutted fish with salt and pepper. Spread the rest of the stuffing inside and then place on the roll of stuffing.
11. Sew up the back of the fish with kitchen twine.
12. Wrap the fish firmly into a kitchen cloth and tie the ends at the head and tail securely.
13. Lay the fish in the previously prepared stock and let it poach gently for about 30 minutes at 90°C/194°F. Test if cooked with a needle. Finally, allow the fish to cool in the liquor.
14. Remove the pike-perch carefully from the liquor and undo the cloth. Remove the skin carefully from both sides, using a sharp knife from between the back of the head and the tail, cutting the skin away in a diagonal line. Remove the layer of brown-coloured fat. Wash over the rest of the surfaces with a brush, using lukewarm water.

Service:

15. Trim the tail fins with scissors. Cut the skinned part between the head and tail into 8 even-sized slices.
16. Cut the lower surfaces of both the head and the tail level, so that they will stand well on the dish, and garnish them with the turned carrot and courgette (zucchini). Use a little fish aspic to fix the garnish to the fish.
17. Arrange the head and tail on a serving dish. Lay the slices of fish in an arc to one side of the dish. On the opposite side place an arc consisting of the filled artichoke bottoms, and arrange the smoked salmon slices artistically in the centre. Serve the yoghurt and chervil sauce separately in a sauceboat.

Beginning at the dorsal fin, remove the backbone

Cut along the backbone, so that the fish can be gutted from above

The beet or spinach leaves are coated with the stuffing and rolled up

The inside of the fish is coated with the stuffing

The leaf-covered roll of stuffing is placed inside the fish to give it its delicate marbling

Finally, the fish is sewn up with kitchen twine

Turbot Stuffed with Salmon

Cool in appearance and nobly presented. this fine dish of turbot could occupy the centre of a buffet table and be admired by all. It combines the delicate salmon stuffing with the firm flesh of the turbot, offering a treat both to the eye and the palate.

Turbot Stuffed with Salmon

To serve 8:

1 Turbot of 2000 gr/4½ lbs	
juice of 1 lemon	
400 gr/14 oz beet leaves or spinach	
150 gr/5 oz salmon fillet	
75 gr/2¾ fl. oz egg white	
100 gr/3½ oz cream	
salt, pepper	
10 ml/⅓ fl. oz Noilly Prat or Pernod	
3 litres/106 fl. oz Court-bouillon (see p. 75)	
2 tomatoes	
100 gr/3½ oz mange-tout (sugar peas/snow peas)	
8 artichoke bottoms with vegetables (see p. 57)	
1 jar quails' eggs	

extra, if necessary:

18 sheets gelatine	
½ litre/19 fl. oz cream	
½ litre/19 fl. oz fish stock	

Time Necessary:

Preparation: 100 minutes
(without cooling time)
Service: 20 minutes

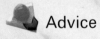 **Advice**

Noilly Prat is a dry white French vermouth which goes very well in fish dishes.

Preparation:

1. First prepare the turbot for poaching. Remove the fins from around the fish, using kitchen scissors, and cutting from head to tail. Cut the tail fin into a semicircle.
2. Now remove the backbone. Lay the turbot with the dark skin uppermost. Somewhere near the centre of the fish running between the head and tail a clear line can be seen, which marks out the two fillets. Open up the fish with a sharp knife, leaving about 2 cm/1" uncut at both head and tail.
3. Now cut between the flesh and backbone to free the fillets to about 2 cm/1" from the outside edges.
4. Using a sharp pointed knife now cut under the backbone, and using the scissors cut the centre away by cutting the ends of the backbone as near the edge as possible. Remove the backbone.
5. Wash the fish thoroughly, both inside and outside, and dry well. Season the inside with lemon juice and salt.
6. Wash the beet leaves or spinach thoroughly. Remove the stalks and any tough centre ribs. Blanch the leaves briefly in boiling salted water and refresh immediately. Dry well using kitchen paper towels.
7. Prepare the salmon stuffing. Cut the salmon up small then pass it through a food processor or blender. Add the cream and egg whites little by little. Season with salt, pepper, and Noilly Prat or Pernod.
8. Lay the turbot, white side down, on the work surface. Turn back the fillets and spread it with about one third of the stuffing. Spread out the beet or spinach leaves on to the stuffing, then cover it with another third of the stuffing. Cover this over with the ends of the leaves, and place the rest of the stuffing on top. Fold the fillets over the top and re-form into its original shape.
9. Dampen a clean kitchen towel well and spread it out. Lay the turbot on it, cut side down, and wrap it up. Place it in a deep oven pan large enough to take the fish and fill with court-bouillon. Poach the fish in the oven at 150°C/300°F for about 35 minutes. Check if cooked, with a needle.
10. Prepare the garnish. Blanch the tomatoes, refresh quickly, then skin them. Cut in half lengthwise and remove the seeds. Cut each half into 4 equal parts.
11. Clean the mange-tout (sugar peas/snow peas) then blanch in boiling salted water and refresh before cutting into diamond shapes.

Begin from the tail when removing the fins

The turbot is cut down the middle to remove the centre bone

Cut close to the bone, then turn back the fillets, and remove the roe

The centre bone is freed using scissors at the outside edge

With the last cut the centre bone can be easily removed

The turbot is filled with several layers of beet or spinach leaves and stuffing

The fish is laid cut-side down on to a dampened kitchen cloth then wrapped up before being poached in a court-bouillon

12. Prepare the artichoke bottoms, adding half a quail's egg, as garnish.
13. Take the turbot from the oven and let it cool in the stock, finally unwrapping it, and with the white side uppermost, place it on a wire cooling rack, until cold.
14. Now the turbot can be coated with a jelly, if wished. Soak the gelatine in cold water, drain it and heat it gently, together with the cream and the fish stock. Keep the mixture in a cool place until almost set.
15. Under the wire cooling rack place an oven tin in order to catch any drips of the jelly which falls off the turbot. Coat the turbot with the jelly, using a small ladle. Repeat the process until the fish is completely and evenly coated. Finally allow the whole to get cold, in a cool place.

Service:

16. Should the fish not be coated with the jelly as above, it can be given a light coat of fish aspic. The fish should then be cut into portions, using a warmed knife. The individual slices can then also be given a coat of fish aspic, if desired.
17. Garnish the fish with the tomatoes and mange-tout. The tomatoes should be placed on the head of the fish in a star shape, with a quail's egg in the centre.
18. The mange-tout should be arranged at the top of the fish in a fan shape. Coat both garnishes with fish aspic.
19. Place the turbot on a silver dish and decorate with the artichoke bottoms.

Court-Bouillon

Preparation:

1. Peel the onions, carrots and celeriac, and slice finely.
2. Wash the parsley, and tie together with kitchen twine.
3. Bring all ingredients except the white wine to the boil and cook for about 12 minutes.
4. Allow to cool, and before use, add the white wine, while heating.

The poached turbot is coated several times with the jelly

It is best to cut the turbot using a warmed knife

2 onions
2 carrots
1 small celeriac
1 bunch parsley
1½ litres/53 fl. oz water
2 dessertspoons salt
250 ml/9 fl. oz white wine

Time Necessary:

Preparation: 20 minutes

Lobster with Green and White Asparagus

Connoisseurs always agree that lobster is the most elegant dish and is always the highlight of the cold buffet. This composition with asparagus presents the tastiest, selected lobster flesh on a piquant salad of finely-diced vegetables.

Lobster with Green and White Asparagus

To serve 8:

1000 gr/2¼ lbs white asparagus	
1000 gr/2¼ lbs green asparagus	
400 gr/14 oz vegetable salad (see p. 133)	
5 lobsters each of 500 gr/18 oz	
2 onions	
2 carrots	
1 teaspoon caraway seeds	
salt, crushed peppercorns	
50 gr/1¾ oz fish aspic	

Sauce:

350 gr/12 oz crème fraîche (soured cream)
100 ml/3½ fl. oz orange juice

To marinate the asparagus

salt and pepper
vinegar, oil

Time Necessary:

Preparation: 1 hr 20 min (without cooling time)
Service: 20 minutes

Preparation:

1. Prepare and cook the asparagus as described on p. 127.
2. In order that the best-looking lobster remains straight while cooking, it should be tied down with twine to a board which is large enough to allow it to be spread out to its full width and length.
3. Bring water to the boil in a pot large enough for the lobsters and the board.
4. Peel and quarter the onion. Wash, peel and cut the carrots into small pieces, adding them with the onion, caraway seeds, some salt, and the crushed peppercorns to the boiling water.
5. Put the lobsters, one by one, into the boiling water, heads first, ensuring that the water remains on the boil.
6. Allow the lobsters to cook for 10 minutes, then let them cool in the liquor.
7. Prepare the presentation lobster to be placed in the centre of the dish. Untie the twine and lay it on its back. With sharp scissors, remove the shell in the area of the tail and remove the flesh. Then turn the lobster over, with the back uppermost.
8. Cut the lobster tail flesh into slices, placing them from head to tail along the back of the lobster. Coat with a little fish aspic, and finally decorate with a few leaves of chervil.
9. Now prepare the other lobsters. Remove the claws from the body with a twisting action and remove the legs.
10. Cut the lobsters into halves, using a large heavy knife, by passing the knife blade between tail and body and cutting lengthwise. Remove the flesh from the bodies and allow to cool.
11. Remove the sac from the head part then scrape out the remainder to be kept for use in the sauce.
12. Wash out the half shells and dry them.
13. Break open the claws on the edge, using the back of a knife, then remove the flesh from within.
14. Cut off the joints above the claws and remove the flesh from these in the same way as above placing it with the flesh from the claws.

The best lobster is bound to a board

The presentation lobster is turned upside-down and the tail-area shell is removed

The tail flesh is cut into slices which will be arranged on the back of the lobster

Service:

15. Fill the lobster half shells with the vegetable salad. Place the halved lobster claws on top, with the red side uppermost.
16. Fill the head space of the lobsters with the remaining flesh from the claws.
17. Garnish each half with a stick of white and green asparagus, tips pointing towards the head.
18. Pass the head contents through a hair sieve for the sauce.
19. Beat together with the soured cream and orange juice to produce a smooth sauce. Season with salt and pepper.
20. Place the presentation lobster in the centre of the dish.
21. Arrange the asparagus below the tail of the lobster in a fan shape using alternating coloured rows.
22. Arrange the halved lobsters to the left and right in a parallel fashion.
23. Sprinkle the asparagus with a mixture of salt, pepper, vinegar and oil.
24. Put the sauce into a sauceboat or a small bowl to be served with the dish.

The claw is removed with a twisting action

The lobster is cut in half by placing the point of the knife between tail and body

The head contents are removed using a teaspoon, and saved for use in the sauce

The claws are cracked with the back of the knife and the flesh removed

The connecting joints are cut with scissors and the flesh removed

MEAT,
SAUSAGES,
POULTRY AND GAME

Substantial Smoked Sausages with Gherkins and Radishes

To serve 8:

1 bunch radishes

4 pairs landjäger sausages

300 gr/11 oz smoked liver sausage

300 gr/11 oz smoked mettwurst

300 gr/11 oz smoked blood sausage

1 small jar gherkins

1 small jar miniature corn-cobs

crisp salad leaves for garnishing

Time Necessary:

Preparation: 15 minutes
Service: 10 minutes

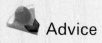 **Advice**

If the dish of sausages is to stay some time in a warm temperature, it is recommended that the skins be left on them.

Preparation:

1. Wash the radishes thoroughly and cut off the roots. Leave about 2 cm/1″ of the stalks, cutting the rest off. Cut the prepared radishes as shown on page 144, and leave to soak in cold water for about 1 hour.
2. Part the landjäger sausages and cut across diagonally in the centre.
3. Cut the other types of sausage into 8 to 10 slices each.

Service:

4. Arrange the slices of sausage on an oval dish. Begin with the blood sausage in the left-hand corner. Follow on with the mettwurst in the same direction.

5. Stack the landjäger inside the mettwurst, pointing outwards, and finish off with the liver sausage, at the bottom.

6. Lay out the salad leaves in the remaining space on the board, and place the gherkins, corn-cobs and radishes thereon, in groups.

Red and White Brawn with Herb Vinaigrette

To serve 8:

1 bunch parsley
1 bunch chervil
1 bunch chives
2 hard-boiled eggs
$\frac{1}{4}$ litre/9 fl. oz oil
5 dessertspoons wine vinegar
salt, pepper
1 bunch radishes
8 slices each of red and white brawn, not too thinly cut
various salad leaves

Time Necessary:

Preparation: 15 minutes
Service: 5 minutes

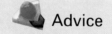 Advice

Serve with
chunky coarse
rye bread.

Preparation:

1. Begin by preparing the herb vinaigrette. Wash the herbs separately and thoroughly.
2. Pull the leaves from the stalks of both parsley and chervil, and chop finely. Finally cut up the chives very finely.
3. Shell the hard-boiled egg, cut it in half, and separate the white from the yolk, cutting each into tiny dice.
4. Mix the oil and vinegar, season with salt and pepper, add the above-mentioned ingredients and mix together.
5. Clean the radishes, wash thoroughly and cut them as described on page 144.

Service:

6. Halve the slices of the red and white brawn and arrange them in the dish, overlapping, one type on each side, following the shape of the dish.
7. Arrange the salad leaves in the centre of the dish, with the radishes on top.
8. Spread some of the herb vinaigrette over the brawn slices, and serve the remainder separately, in a sauceboat.

Salted Brisket (Corned Beef) with Green Sauce

To serve 8:

800 gr/28 oz sliced boiled salt brisket (corned beef)

green sauce (see p. 168)

some crisp salad leaves

sweet-sour pickled vegetables (see p. 40)

Time Necessary:

Preparation: 10 minutes
Service: 15 minutes

Preparation:

1. Lay the beef slices exactly in line together, so that any excess fat may be removed in one go and leave an even amount to show on the dish.
2. Clean and wash the salads and allow to drain thoroughly.

Service:

3. Pour the green sauce into the dish to cover completely the bottom surface. Lay the sliced beef on top in an arc, following the shape of the dish, with each slice overlapping.
4. Lay out the salad leaves in the remaining space and arrange the sweet-sour pickled vegetables on top. Serve with crisp white French sticks.

Sausage Selection with
Stuffed Cucumber

Preparation:

1. First prepare the cucumber. Wash it and cut the bottom so that it will stand level.
2. On the top side, about 4 cm/1½″ from each end, make an oblique cut downwards, about 2 cm/1″ deep, and with a straight cut, remove the top section. Remove the seeds with a teaspoon.
3. Finally, blanch the cucumber, momentarily, in salted boiling water.
4. Pour out the mixed pickles, allow to drain well, and cut into small pieces, if necessary. Arrange decoratively in the cucumber.

Service:

5. Place the cucumber across the left upper corner of the serving dish. Arrange the bierschinken in a circle at the right upper corner.

6. Beginning with the bierwurst, lay out a semi-circle from the cucumber, following with the jagdwurst and mortadella.

7. Roll the salami into cone shapes and arrange between the cucumber and the bierwurst.

To serve 8:

1 salad cucumber

salt

1 small jar mixed vinegar pickles

200 gr/7 oz sliced bierschinken

200 gr/7 oz sliced bierwurst

200 gr/7 oz sliced jagdwurst

200 gr/7 oz sliced mortadella

200 gr/7 oz sliced salami

Time Necessary:

Preparation: 15 minutes
Service: 10 minutes

 Advice

Serve this dish with coarse types of bread, butter and hot mustard.

Assorted Country-Style Cold Meat Platter without Pork Products

To serve 8:

4 large white turnips

vinegar

2 tomatoes

1 onion

1 can sweetcorn

salt, pepper

oil

200 gr/7 oz roast turkey breast, or smoked guineafowl breast, sliced

200 gr/7 oz sliced corned beef

200 gr/7 oz sliced beef bierschinken

200 gr/7 oz sliced poultry sausage

Time Necessary:

Preparation: 30 minutes
Service: 10 minutes

 Advice

Serve this dish with green sauce and mixed-grain bread.

The turnips are hollowed out with a pommes parisienne cutter

Preparation:

1. First of all prepare the garnish. Peel the turnips and cut them across into two. Cut the undersides flat and make them all the same height. Hollow out the centre using a pommes parisienne cutter.
2. Place the half turnips in boiling salted water with a dash of vinegar, blanch them briefly and allow to cool.
3. Blanch the tomatoes, refresh and skin. Finally cut across, remove the seeds, and cut the flesh into fine dice.
4. Peel the onion and cut into fine dice. Drain off the corn, drain well and mix with the onion. Season with salt, pepper, vinegar and oil to make a piquant salad.
5. Mix in the tomato carefully, then dress the salad into the prepared turnip halves.

Service:

6. Arrange the filled turnip halves in an arc from the top left corner of the serving dish to the top right corner.
7. Then arrange 4 slices of the turkey breast overlapping from the turnip halves to the outside bottom corners. Place the sliced corned beef at the centre bottom in an arc.

The salad is filled into the turnip halves

8. Arrange an arc of slices of beef bierschinken at the top of the dish.

9. Arrange another arc, of poultry sausage, beneath, just touching the turnip halves.

Lombard Delight

To serve 8:

400 gr/14 oz cushion or topside of veal
1 bunch chives
juice of 1 lemon
100 ml/3½ fl. oz olive oil
coarse salt
black pepper
1 radicchio
400 gr/14 oz mushrooms
8 black olives
2 tomatoes

Time Necessary:

Prepare the day before
Preparation: 25 minutes
Marination: 1 day
Service: 15 minutes

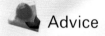 Advice

Serve Italian flat bread with this dish (see page 154).

Preparation:

1. Leave the veal in the deep freezer for a little time to firm it up, so that it may be more easily sliced thinly.
2. Wash the chives thoroughly, dry off well, then cut finely and mix with the oil and lemon juice. Season the dressing with salt and pepper.
3. Pour the dressing into a deep plate.
4. Cut the veal across the grain into thin slices, and lay it into the dressing.
5. Cover the meat with the dressing, then lay on more, making sure that each layer is covered with the dressing. Finish with a layer of dressing, then leave the meat to marinate for one day.

Service:

6. On the next day, clean and wash the radicchio, drain well and arrange on a glass plate.
7. Arrange the marinated veal on top.
8. Clean the mushrooms and slice finely, then arrange over the top of the veal.
9. Garnish the dish with the tomatoes and the olives.

Vitello Tonnato (Sliced Veal in Tuna-Fish Sauce)

To serve 8:

1 onion

2 bayleaves

1 clove

1000 gr/2¼ lbs cushion or topside of veal

200 gr/7 oz tuna fish without oil

5 anchovy fillets

100 gr/3½ oz mayonnaise (see p. 168)

juice of 2 lemons

For garnish:

2 hard-boiled eggs

1 dessertspoon capers

vinegar-pickled gherkins

black and green olives

Time Necessary:

Preparation: 60 minutes (without cooling time)
Service: 10 minutes
Marination: 5 hours

 Advice

Serve with a green side-salad and fresh crusty bread. This dish is specially good for a summer buffet.

Preparation:

1. Peel the onion and fix the bayleaf to it with the cloves.
2. Halve the cushion of veal lengthwise and tie with kitchen twine in order that the meat will retain its shape while cooking.
3. Put the meat and the onion into salted water and simmer for 45 minutes over a low heat. Check if cooked, with a needle. Allow to cool in the cooking liquor.
4. While the meat is cooking, make the sauce, by making a purée of the tuna, anchovy fillets, mayonnaise and lemon juice with a food processor, or liquidiser. If the sauce is too thick, add a little of the cooking liquor.

Service:

5. Cut the cold meat into thin slices, and arrange fan-wise around an edged dish.
6. Pour the sauce over the meat, then place the dish in the refrigerator for at least 5 hours.
7. Before serving, decorate the dish with the hard-boiled eggs, capers, gherkins and olives.

Italian Ham and Sausages Specialities with Filled Courgettes (Zucchini)

To serve 8:

8 small courgettes (zucchini)	
3 tomatoes	
1 large aubergine (eggplant)	
2 dessertspoons olive oil	
1 teaspoon tomato purée	
salt, pepper	
a little vinegar	
200 gr/7 oz sliced mortadella sausage	
200 gr/7 oz sliced Parma ham	
200 gr/7 oz sliced coppa (cured neck of pork)	
200 gr/7 oz sliced Italian salami	

Time Necessary:

Preparation: 40 minutes
Service: 10 minutes

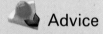

Advice

Serve these Italian specialities with French Sticks and green and black olives.

Preparation:

1. Wash the courgettes (zucchini) and cut off the ends at an angle. Cut off the tops at three-quarter height, leaving a little at the ends, then scoop out the flesh using a pommes parisienne cutter. Keep 8 of the best balls for further use, and cut the rest into $\frac{1}{4}''$ dice.
2. Blanch the courgette pieces, and the balls only very briefly in boiling salted water, then refresh and drain well.

3. Wash, blanch and skin the tomatoes. Finally halve them, remove the seeds and cut them into fine dice. Carry out the same procedures for the aubergine.
4. Heat the olive oil in a pan. Add the aubergine and diced courgette, together with the tomato purée. Fry off lightly, then remove from the pan.
5. Season well with salt and pepper. When cold, add the tomato dice.
6. Fill the salad into the prepared courgettes and garnish with the courgette balls.

Service:

7. Place the courgettes at an angle from the bottom left to top right of the serving dish.
8. Halve the slices of mortadella and overlap them, folded, and with the points outwards arrange them above the courgettes.
9. Arrange the Parma ham between the mortadella and the courgettes.
10. Arrange the coppa in a half circle below the courgettes.

Hollow out the courgettes

Fill the prepared salad into the courgettes

11. Finally, arrange the salami between the coppa and the courgettes.

Pork Loin with Prunes and Rolled Smoked Pork Loin

To serve 8:

1200 gr/2¾ lbs pork loin, on the bone

1000 gr/2¼ lbs smoked pork loin (Kasseler rippenspeer), on the bone

125 gr/4 oz stoned prunes

salt, pepper, oil for frying

1 carrot

1 cauliflower (500 gr/1¼ lbs)

2 broccoli (240 gr/8 oz)

2 apples (Granny Smith)

1 lemon

1 jar pickled fruits

200 gr/7 oz meat aspic

Time Necessary:

Pre-heat the oven to 200°C/400°F
Preparation: 60 minutes (without cooling time)
Service: 15 minutes

Preparation:

1. Prepare the meat for roasting. Scrape clean the bone ends on both joints of meat.
2. Using a long, pointed knife, make a hole right through the centre of the eye of the meat in the pork loin, pressing the flesh outwards, filling this hole with stoned prunes.
3. Finally tie both sorts of meat with kitchen twine so that they keep their shape, while cooking.
4. In order to reduce the salt content of the smoked pork loin, blanch it in boiling water for about ten minutes, before roasting.
5. While blanching the above, season the pork loin with salt and pepper.
6. Fry off both meats in oil in a pan and roast in an oven heated to 200°C/400°F until cooked, for about 35 minutes. Allow to cool thoroughly.
7. Meanwhile, prepare the garnish. Clean and wash the vegetables thoroughly. Peel the carrots and slice them, using a corrugated decorating knife. Break the cauliflower and broccoli into florets.
8. Blanch the vegetables singly, by type, in boiling salted water, leaving them crisp, then drain and allow to get cold.
9. Remove the core from the apples with an apple corer. Cut the tops and bottoms from the apples, so they will stand level. Finally, cut them across to give eight equal height pieces. Hollow these out more with a round cutter.
10. Blanch the apple bases for about 15 seconds in boiling water to which some lemon juice has been added, then refresh quickly and drain well.
11. Drain the pickled fruits and divide them out into the apple halves.

Service:

12. Now remove the flesh in one piece from two-thirds of each type of meat, leaving about 1 cm/½" thickness of flesh on the bones and without separating the ribs.
13. On the ribs, in place of the removed flesh, divide and arrange the prepared vegetables, and give them a light coat of meat aspic.
14. Cut the removed flesh into 8 equal slices, and coat them also with aspic.
15. Arrange both show pieces at an angle to one another, with the bones pointing outwards at the upper part of the serving dish.
16. Arrange the sliced meats in a half circle overlapping each other, starting from the foot of the show pieces and running outwards.
17. Arrange the apple halves in a half circle below the sliced meats. Should there be any excess vegetable garnish, this may be placed between the two show pieces.

The pork loin is prepared for stuffing

The pork loin is stuffed with the prunes

This is how the flesh is removed from the ribs

Replacing the removed flesh with the vegetable garnish

Assorted Roast Meats with Stuffed Dill Pickles

To serve 8:

500 gr/18 oz beef for roasting

500 gr/18 oz pork loin, boned

500 gr/18 oz topside or cushion of veal

salt, pepper

oil for frying

1 small jar mixed pickles

8 dill pickles

green sauce (see p. 168)

remoulade sauce (see p. 169)

Time necessary:

Preparation: 50 minutes
(without cooling time)
Service: 15 minutes

Preparation:

1. First prepare the meat for roasting. Remove any skin or sinews, if necessary. Wash the pieces of meat under running water, then dry well. Tie into shape with kitchen twine.
2. Season each piece of meat and fry off all over separately in hot oil.
3. Place all the joints on a grid in an oven preheated to 200°C/400°F and roast until cooked. The beef will take about 20/30 minutes according to thickness, the pork loin and veal about 25 minutes. Check if cooked with a meat thermometer. The beef should register 60/70°C/140/158°F on the inside, the pork loin and veal should register 85/90°C/185/194°F.
4. Allow the meat to cool thoroughly.
5. For the garnish, pour out the mixed pickles, cut smaller, if necessary and finally, drain off well. Cut the tops from the dill pickles to form lids, remove the seeds, and fill with the mixed pickles.

Service:

6. Slice the cold meats with a sharp knife. Do not cut the roast beef too thinly.
7. Place the dill pickles at an angle across the centre of the serving dish, laying the roast meats to either side. Fold the roast beef lengthwise, and arrange at the edge of the dish, overlapping each slice.

Tie the joints with kitchen twine to keep them in shape while roasting

The meat must be completely cold before slicing

8. Now arrange the roast veal above the dill pickles. Overlap the slices around following the top edge of the dish in one row. The remaining slices should be arranged into rosettes and placed between the sliced veal and the dill pickles, to fill the gap.

Make the veal rosettes using the thumb and forefinger

9. Finally fold the roast pork slices together and lay them between the roast beef and the dill pickles, slightly overlapping.
10. Serve the sauces in sauceboats separately.

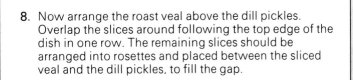

Raw and Cooked Ham with Various Melons

To serve 8 to 10:

1 honeydew melon
1 Ogen melon
1 cantaloupe melon
500 gr/18 oz sliced cooked ham
500 gr/18 oz sliced raw ham

Time Necessary:

Preparation: 20 minutes
Service: 15 minutes

Preparation:

1. Halve the honeydew melon lengthwise and remove the seeds with a teaspoon. Cut each melon half, according to size into 8 to 10 equal segments and remove the skin.
2. Cut the Ogen melon across Vandyke-style (zig-zag) at two-thirds of its height. Remove the seeds as above.
3. Halve the cantaloupe melon and remove the seeds. Cut out all the flesh into balls, using a pommes parisienne cutter, placing the balls into the prepared Ogen melon half. Set the "lid" of the melon on top at a skew.

Service:

4. Arrange the segments of honeydew melon around the edge of a round dish, then lay inside the slices of

cooked ham, folded in half. Inside these arrange the slices of raw ham, also folded, overlapping each other. Finish with a rosette of one slice of raw ham.

5. Place the filled Ogen melon in the centre of the dish.

Ham Mousse with Filled Courgettes (Zucchini)

To serve 8:

12 sheets gelatine

500 gr/18 oz sliced cooked ham

100 gr/3½ oz sliced raw ham

200 gr/7 oz poultry sauce (see p. 174)

20 ml/¾ fl. oz Madeira or port

200 gr/7 oz double cream

2 courgettes (zucchini)

2 carrots

1 small celeriac

4 stuffed olives

salt, pepper

vinegar, oil

100 gr/3½ oz meat aspic

Time Necessary:

Prepare the previous day
Preparation: 1 hr 10 min
(without cooling time)
Service: 20 minutes

 Advice

This dish can be made using more raw or cooked ham if desired. The recipe for ham mousse can also be used for other meats.

Preparation:

1. Soak the gelatine in cold water until soft, then drain off well.
2. Take two slices from the cooked ham and reserve for the garnish. Cut both the raw and cooked ham very small and pass twice through a mincing machine fitted with a fine plate.
3. Finally, mix well with the poultry sauce and pass through a hair sieve.
4. Warm the drained gelatine until dissolved. Beat into the ham mixture with a whisk and season with the Madeira or port.
5. Allow the mixture to cool until it starts to thicken.
6. Meanwhile beat the cream until stiff, and finally line the base of the mould to be used with greaseproof paper.
7. When the ham mixture begins to set, fold in the cream.
8. Take off 2 dessertspoons of the mousse and set aside, the rest being put into the prepared mould and allowed to set in a cold place for at least one day.
9. Quarter the reserved slices of ham, make them into cornets and fill with the reserved ham mousse. Allow them also to set in a cold place.
10. On the next day, prepare the vegetables for the garnish. Cut the courgettes (zucchini) into 4 equal size pieces and hollow them out. Finally, blanch them briefly in boiling salted water.

11. Wash and peel the carrots and celeriac.
12. Cut off 8 thin slices from the carrots and cut them around, using a fluted cutter.
13. Using a small ball cutter cut out small balls of carrot and celeriac, and blanch these in boiling salted water.
14. Halve the stuffed olives and press them into the ham cornets, round side inwards.
15. Place a carrot slice on each of the ham cornets.
16. Drain the vegetable balls well and season them with salt, pepper, oil and vinegar, then fill into the courgette bases.

Service:

17. In order to turn out the mould easily, run the blade of a knife around the edge, then turn out the mould and remove the paper from the base. Glaze with meat aspic, if desired.
18. Cut the mousse into 8 equal portions, using a hot knife. Decorate each portion with one of the ham cornets.
19. Arrange the individual portions on a dish in a circle. Arrange the courgette bases in a ring around the outside of the mousse.

Use a pommes parisienne cutter to remove the flesh from the courgette sections

Use a small ball cutter to make the balls from the carrot

Roast Beef Dish with Stuffed Eggs and Baby Fennel

The presentation piece of roast beef is garnished in this way

To serve 8:

1600 gr/4½ lbs beef for roasting (topside)

4 small baby fennel

2 carrots

2 broccoli florets

salt, pepper

vinegar, oil

4 tomatoes

4 hard-boiled eggs

150 gr/5¼ oz butter

2 teaspoons mustard

green stuffed olives

Time Necessary:

Pre-heat the oven to
200°C/400°F
Preparation: 1 hr 10 min
(without cooling time)
Service: 30 minutes

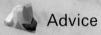 ## Advice

Eggs should not be placed directly on to a silver or silver-plated dish as they cause oxidation and blackening of the dish. The best remedy is to place each half egg on a slice of cucumber, or a cut out round of bread. The dish can also be protected with a thin layer of plain aspic jelly.

Preparation:

1. Prepare and roast the beef as described on p. 96.
2. For the garnish, clean and wash the baby fennel and halve from the root. Cut a little from the underneath so that the fennel halves will stand at an angle.
3. Hollow out the fennel halves a little on the top side. Wash and peel the carrots and cut into ¼" dice.
4. Blanch the carrots, fennel, and broccoli in boiling salted water.
5. Drain the carrots well, then season them with salt, pepper, vinegar and oil. Finally, fill the carrot salad into the fennel halves.
6. Blanch the tomatoes, skin them, halve them lengthwise and remove the seeds, then cut each half into 3 or 4 according to size.
7. Halve the hard-boiled eggs lengthwise. Pass the yolks through a hair sieve. Mix them with butter and mustard, then season them with salt and pepper.
8. Wash and dry the egg white halves.
9. Pipe the egg yolk mixture into the egg white halves using a star tube. Garnish the egg halves with a tomato segment and a slice of olive.

Service:

10. Slice half of the roast beef.
11. Garnish the remaining piece of roast beef with the tomato segments and the broccoli florets.
12. Place the decorated piece of roast beef in the upper right corner of the serving dish, pointing diagonally downwards.
13. Arrange the slices of roast beef folded lengthwise in two rows running from the show piece diagonally downwards to the opposite corner.
14. Arrange the stuffed egg halves in an arc below the roast beef, and the fennel halves above, in the same way.

Chicken Galantine with Smoked Turkey Breast and Glazed Leeks

Chicken Galantine with Smoked Turkey Breast and Glazed Leeks

To serve 8:

1 roasting chicken, drawn, about 1000 gr/2¼ lbs

salt, pepper

mixed herbs (commercial product)

40 ml/1½ fl. oz brandy

100 gr/3½ oz cooked ox-tongue

100 gr/3½ oz cooked ham

150 gr/5¼ oz veal

150 gr/5¼ oz pork

100 gr/3½ oz bacon

125 ml/4 fl. oz cream

2000 ml/70 fl. oz chicken stock

3 bunches young leeks

100 gr/3½ oz sugar

4 dessertspoons vinegar

some water

For the garnish of the galantine:

1 leek

1 carrot

200 gr/7 oz meat aspic

200 gr/7 oz sliced roast turkey breast

Time Necessary:

Prepare the previous day
Preparation time: 2 hr 50 min (without cooling time)
Service: 15 minutes

Preparation:

1. Cut off the winglet at the second joint from the tip.
2. Cut round the skin on the leg above the foot joint so that the sinews can be withdrawn.
3. Using the back of the knife, break the bone through and draw out the bone together with the sinews from the leg. If necessary use the knife to help free the sinews.
4. Lay the chicken on its breast and cut through the skin to the bone, along the centre of the back from neck to tail.
5. Beginning on the right side, free the flesh from the rib cage. Cut off the wing bones at the joint freeing as much flesh as possible in that way, then repeat for the leg bones.
6. Now free the flesh along the side of the breastbone.
7. Now repeat for the left-hand side of the bird.
8. Remove the carcase from the flesh.
9. Lay the flesh out evenly, and remove both wing bones, by pushing the bone inside, as far as possible, freeing the flesh as you go, and removing any remnants from inside by scraping with the knife.
10. In the same way, free the flesh from the leg bones.
11. Now rearrange the bird so that the skin covers the correct part of the flesh.
12. Make a couple of light cuts into the flesh of the legs, from the inside, so that they do not twist, while the bird is being poached, and to keep the flesh thickness even throughout the galantine.
13. Season the prepared bird with salt, pepper and mixed herbs together with a few drops of brandy, and leave to marinate.
14. Prepare the stuffing. Cut the ox-tongue and cooked ham into tiny dice and put in a cold place.
15. Take the veal, pork and bacon and cut up small, then season with salt, pepper, mixed herbs and a few drops of brandy, and allow to marinate for a little.
16. Finally, pass the veal, pork and bacon individually twice through a mincing machine fitted with a fine blade, or another type of machine which will produce a purée, and put in a cold place.
17. Mix the veal and pork together well, preferably over ice. Little by little, add the bacon. Finally mix in the cream. Season with salt, pepper, mixed herbs and brandy.
18. Finally, mix in the diced ham and tongue.

Cut off the winglet at the second joint

Using the back of the knife, break the bone through and draw out the bone together with the sinews from the leg

The chicken is laid on its back and the flesh is freed from the carcase along one side

Now the flesh can be removed from the carcase

The wing bones are removed by pushing them inwards and easing the flesh from them there

In order to keep the flesh an even thickness, the flesh of the legs is cut across

19. Fill the chicken with the stuffing and then get it ready for poaching, by spreading the stuffing out evenly over the whole surface.
20. Starting from the side containing the two legs, roll up the chicken tightly. Wrap it well in suitable clingfilm, close up the ends and tie in a regular shape with kitchen twine.
21. Poach the galantine in chicken stock at about 80°C/176°F for about 1 hour, and let it cool in the liquor.
22. On the following day prepare the garnish. Clean and wash the leeks and cut them into 8 cm/3" lengths.
23. Heat the sugar in a pan and let it caramelise lightly. Deglaze the pan with vinegar and fill up with water. Cook out after seasoning with salt.
24. Cook the leeks in this stock and allow them to get cold.
25. Meanwhile, unwrap the galantine and cut off 8 even slices. Coat both the slices and the remaining piece of galantine with meat aspic, if desired.
26. Halve and wash the remaining leek. Peel and wash the carrot.
27. From the green of the leek cut two long strips, cut the remainder into diamond shapes.
28. Cut the carrot into slices and cut them into even sized shapes using a round fluted cutter.
29. Blanch both the leek and carrot.
30. Using these items, make a flower to decorate the galantine. .

Service:

31. With the cut side pointing towards the centre, arrange the galantine, at an angle, on an oval serving dish, in the left upper corner.
32. Arrange the slices of galantine in a half circle from the whole piece to the top right hand corner, lightly overlapping.
33. Lay the turkey breast slices below the galantine, following the same arc.

34. Arrange the glazed leeks in a pile, with the green parts at the top, above the slices of galantine. Serve Cumberland sauce separately.

The stuffing is spread over the top surface of the chicken

Roast Duck with Mango Segments

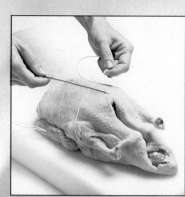

The duck is trussed to keep its shape during roasting

To serve 8:

1 duck, drawn, about 1200 gr/3½ lbs

salt, pepper

oil for frying

4 duck breasts each 200 gr/7 oz

4 sheets gelatine

200 gr/7 oz Waldorf salad (see p. 134)

2 oranges

100 gr/3½ oz meat aspic

300 gr/11 oz grapes

some angelica

3 mangos

Time Necessary:

Pre-heat the oven to 200°C/400°F
Preparation: 1 hr 10 min (without cooling)
Service: 40 minutes

 Advice

Angelica is the candied stalk of the angelica-root. This is a medicinal and flavouring plant used for making liqueurs, though today it is mainly used in the decoration of sweet items. It is freely available in good grocers and delicatessens.

1. Prepare the duck for roasting. Remove any traces of feathers and wash the bird inside and out. Finally drain and dry off, then season with salt and pepper.
2. Truss the duck using kitchen twine and trussing needle, in order to keep the bird in the desired shape during cooking, passing the twine through both thighs and wings tying both ends together.
3. Fry off both breasts in oil, then lay the bird on its back, and roast in an oven heated to 200°C/400°F until cooked, about 45 minutes.
4. Now prepare the duck breasts for roasting. If necessary remove any sinews from the flesh side, then season with salt and pepper, and lay the breasts skin side down into the frying pan.
5. After 5 minutes, turn the breasts over and cook the other sides for a further 5 minutes, then let both the duck breasts and duck get cold.

Service:

6. Carefully remove the kitchen twine from the duck, and cut the bottom side of the duck level so that it will stand level.
7. Bone out the breasts from the whole duck, and carve into 12 even-sized slices.
8. Soften the gelatine in cold water, then drain it off well, and warm it until it is dissolved.
9. Bind the Waldorf salad with the dissolved gelatine and rebuild the original shape of the duck breast with it on the carcase.
10. Now lay the slices of duck breast on top alternately left and right sides, so that each overlap, beginning with the smallest slices, at the back. Use some almost cold aspic to hold the slices better, if needed.
11. Fillet the oranges, and drain off the fillets well.
12. Place 2 fillets opposite each other on the top of the duck, in the centre, starting from the front to the back. Place a half grape on each pair of fillets.
13. Cut diamonds from the angelica and place these to left and right of the grapes.
14. The garnished duck may be coated lightly with more meat aspic, if desired.
15. Now cut up the duck breasts into slices, but against the grain of the flesh.
16. Cut the mangos into even-sized segments, remove from the stone, and peel.

Bone out the breasts from each side of the breastbone

17. Place the duck in the centre of the serving dish with the tail end up against the top edge, so as to leave space below the neck end. Lay the breast slices at an angle on each side of the duck, lightly overlapping each other.
18. Arrange the mango slices below the duck, fanning outwards from the centre, with a small bunch of the remaining grapes in the centre. Serve this dish with orange sauce to achieve full flavour.

Fix the duck breast slices using small skewers or cocktail sticks, while first arranging them

Best-end and Medallions of Veal with Vegetable Terrine

To serve 8:

2500 gr/5 lbs 8 oz best-end of veal (loin of veal)	
salt, pepper	
oil for roasting	
400 gr/14 oz fillet of veal	
2 courgettes (zucchini)	
20 mushroom heads	
juice of 2 lemons	
50 gr/1¾ oz fine calves' liver sausage	
40 gr/1½ oz butter	
10 ml/⅓ fl. oz port	
200 gr/7 oz meat aspic jelly	
vegetable terrine (see p. 43)	

Time Needed:

Pre-heat the oven to
180°C/350°F
Preparation: 1 hr 30 min
(without cooling)
Service: 40 minutes

Preparation:

1. Begin with the preparation of the meat. Clean off the ends of the bones from the best end of veal, removing any meat and tendons.
2. Tie up the best-end with kitchen twine, season with salt and pepper, and fry off the meat-side evenly in oil.
3. Finish off the cooking in an oven heated to 180°C/350°F. Roasting time will be about 60 minutes. Test with a needle after this time. The juices should still be a light pink colour.
4. Remove any fat and tendons from the fillet. Season it and roast it in the oven with the best end, turning it frequently. Cooking time is about 15 minutes at 180°C/350°F. Allow both pieces of meat to cool.
5. Meanwhile, prepare the garnish. Wash the courgettes (zucchini) and cut them into lengths of 3 cm/1¼". Cut these into quarters lengthwise then round them off (turn), afterwards blanching them in boiling salted water, leaving them still crisp.
6. Turn the mushrooms, cook in water to which lemon juice has been added, and allow to cool.
7. Beat the calves' liver sausage together with the butter, using a whisk, and flavour with the port.
8. Prepare the best end and fillet for decoration. Cut the fillet on the slant into eight even-sized medallions.
9. Fill a piping bag fitted with a star tube with the liver/butter paste and pipe a rosette at the top of each medallion of fillet, and garnish with a turned mushroom and turned piece of courgette (zucchini).

Service:

10. Take out the best end and cut it into eight even-sized slices.
11. If desired, glaze the medallions and slices of veal with a coat of almost cool meat aspic.
12. Cut the vegetable terrine into eight even slices, then cut these in half.
13. Beginning with those on the bone, lay out the slices of best end from the top left-hand side of the platter, towards the centre, in a curve, overlapping each slice, with the skin side uppermost.
14. Lay the decorated slices of fillet at an angle along the top edge of the platter with the last two at the bottom right.
15. Lay the slices of vegetable terrine around the outside of the slices of best end, overlapping.
16. Finally, lay out the rest of the mushrooms and courgettes (zucchini) in the bottom left-hand corner of the platter.

 Advice

The vegetable terrine should be made on the previous day.

The mushrooms must be turned so that the top resembles a spiral

The courgettes are turned so as to leave some peel on each piece

Medallions of Veal, Beef, Pork and Venison Fillets

The medallions are tied to that they will remain round while cooking

To serve 8:

400 gr/14 oz pork fillet

400 gr/14 oz veal fillet

salt, pepper

oil for frying

400 gr/14 oz beef fillet

400 gr/14 oz venison fillet

160 gr/5½ oz butter

40 ml/1½ fl. oz madeira or brandy

1 orange

100 gr/3½ oz calves' sweetbreads (thymus)

120 gr/4 oz broccoli

8 button mushrooms

juice of 1 lemon

1 courgette (zucchini)

2 slices pineapple

8 walnut kernels

chopped pistachio nuts

Time Necessary:

Pre-heat the oven to 200°C/400°F
Preparation: 1 hr 40 min (without cooling time)
Service: 5 minutes

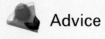 **Advice**

With these medallions serve both orange and Tyrolean sauces.

Preparation:

1. Start with the preparation of the fillets. Cut the veal and pork fillets into 10 medallions.
2. Tie the medallions with kitchen twine. Season with salt and pepper, and fry off in a pan in oil for about 5 minutes, leaving them still underdone.
3. Take the medallions out of the pan, and allow them to cool off.
4. Tie the beef and venison fillets with kitchen twine to keep their shape, season with salt and pepper, then fry them off in the pan, in oil. Transfer to the oven, heated to 200°C/400°F and roast until cooked. This will take about 8 minutes.
5. Remove the fillets from the oven pan and allow them to cool thoroughly.
6. After cooling, cut the beef and venison fillets diagonally into 8 even medallions. The trimmings from the ends should be put to one side.
7. Now prepare the garnish. Take the trimmings from the beef and venison fillets, together with 2 veal and pork medallions, putting each separately through the food processor together with 40 gr/1½ oz butter. Season each type with a dash of cognac or madeira, salt and pepper.
8. Peel and fillet the orange.
9. Skin and clean the calves' sweetbreads then season with salt and pepper, before wrapping into a roll in suitable clingfilm. Seal the ends and cook this roll in salted water for 5 minutes.
10. Wash the broccoli, divide it into 8 equal florets, then blanch it in boiling salted water.
11. Turn the mushrooms, then cook briefly in water to which lemon juice has been added.
12. Cut the courgette (zucchini) into 3 cm/1¼″ lengths. Cut these lengthwise into three and cut into an oval shape, leaving some skin left on. Finally blanch briefly in boiling salted water.
13. Peel and quarter the pineapple slices.
14. Garnish the medallions. Remove the twine from the veal and pork medallions, then pipe each medallion with a rosette of its own accompanying mousse, using a star tube.
15. Garnish the venison medallions with an orange segment and a half walnut.
16. Unwrap the calves' sweetbreads and cut into 8 even slices. Garnish the veal medallions each with one of these and a floret of broccoli.
17. Garnish the beef medallions with the courgettes and mushroom heads.
18. Garnish the pork medallions with the pineapple slice quarters and pistachio nuts.

The twine is removed and the mousse piped on top

Service:

19. Arrange the venison medallions on the serving dish in a line to run from top right hand corner to bottom left.
20. Arrange the pork medallions above these and the veal medallions below.
21. Finally arrange the beef medallions above and below, parallel to the others in the remaining space.

Venison Ham with Hare Pie

The fillets lie under the rib bones

To serve 8:-

2 legs of hare

200 gr/7 oz veal

200 gr/7 oz neck of pork

salt, pepper

mixed herbs (commercial product)

some brandy

350–400 gr/12–14 oz saddle of hare

oil for frying

200 gr/7 oz cream

50 gr/1¾ oz diced ham

50 gr/1¾ oz pistachio nuts

200 gr/7 oz thinly sliced unsmoked bacon

Pastry:

400 gr/14 oz flour

pinch salt

140 gr/5 oz firm dripping

some water

2 egg yolks

250 gr/9 oz meat aspic

400 gr/14 oz sliced venison ham

Time Necessary:

Pre-heat the oven to 250°C/480°F
Preparation: 1 hr 50 min (without cooling time)
Service: 10 minutes.

Preparation:

1. Remove the skin from the legs of hare, and bone them out. Remove any coarse sinews, then cut the meat into small dice.
2. Cut up the pork and veal separately into small dice. Marinate in pepper, mixed herbs and brandy together with the diced hare meat.
3. Cut out the eye of the loin from the hare and remove the skin.
4. Cut out the fillets from beneath the rib cage and add these to the marinated hare meat.
5. Cut the loin fillets to the length of the pie mould. Season them with salt, pepper, and fry off all round in hot oil. Take them out of the pan and allow to cool.
6. Purée the marinated meats individually in a food processor or blender, with the addition of salt, pepper, mixed herbs and cream.
7. Beat the puréed meats together, seasoning them again, if necessary. Add the diced ham and pistachio nuts. Allow the filling to get cold.
8. If desired, roll the fried-off hare fillets in unsmoked bacon.
9. Now prepare the pastry. Sieve the flour and add the salt.
10. Cut the hard dripping into dice, put into the flour, then rub in to form a crumb.
11. Add the cold water and knead the whole together to make a dough, but do not knead too long, or it will become tough. The dough can then be rolled out.
12. Cut off three-quarters of the dough and roll this out into a rectangle 5 mm/¼" thick and large enough to allow for the bottom of the mould as well as the sides and an overlap of 2 cm/1" on each side. Line the mould with this.
13. Line the inside of the pastry with slices of unsmoked bacon and place half of the filling into the bottom, pressing it well down.
14. Now lay in both loin fillets lengthwise, and fill with the remaining filling, to the top.
15. Flatten the top surface with a spatula, and bang the filled mould down hard several times to get rid of any possible air bubbles in the filling.
16. Close the overlapping ends of the bacon over the top of the filling, so that a complete layer of bacon shows at the top.

The pie mould is lined with pastry and sliced unsmoked bacon

17. Cut off the overlapping dough on the short sides. Pull the dough on the long sides inwards towards the centre so that the top will not be too thick at the edges.
18. Beat the egg yolks with a little water, and paint the top of the dough with it.
19. Roll the remaining dough out into a rectangle, and lay it on to the pie, pressing it well down at the edges and cutting off the surplus with a knife. Press down the edges again.
20. Using a round cutter, cut two holes into the top of the pie and decorate these and the top using pastry remains. Paint the whole top of the pie with the egg yolk mixture. Make two chimneys from aluminium foil to place in the holes in order to let steam escape and to avoid the top splitting.
21. Bake the pie in an oven heated to 250°C/480°F for 10 minutes, then reduce the heat to 180°C/350°F for a further 30 minutes. Cover the top surface of the pie with aluminium foil if it shows signs of getting too brown. Check that the centre is cooked with a needle.
22. Take the pie out of the oven and let it cool a little so that the top will sink somewhat, while settling.
23. Now fill the whole of the top space with almost setting meat aspic, filling the pie by means of the chimneys until it overflows.
24. Let the pie get cold, then finally turn it out of the mould, closing up any cracks in the pastry with cold butter.

Service:

25. Cut one end off the pie, then cut 8 equal-sized slices from it.
26. Place the pie in the upper left-hand corner of the serving dish, with the cut side pointing towards the centre.
27. Arrange 5 slices of pie, slightly overlapping, from the pie to the bottom right corner.
28. Halve the remaining 3 slices and place these in the top right hand corner of the dish, parallel to the direction of the pie, and slightly overlapping.
29. Arrange the sliced venison ham in rows between the slices of pie, and also in the free space at the bottom left-hand corner.

The middle layer of the pie consists of the fried-off loin fillets

The overlapping bacon is then covered over the filling

Chimneys made from aluminium foil serve to allow steam to escape from the pie

Loin of Venison with Fresh Figs and Stuffed Pears

To serve 8:

2000 gr/4½ lbs saddle of venison
salt, pepper
oil
4 pears
sugar
100 ml/3½ fl. oz white wine
juice of 1 lemon
160 gr/5½ oz chanterelle mushrooms
1 onion
vinegar
some lamb's lettuce
8 fresh figs
100 gr/3½ oz fine calves' liver sausage
70 gr/2½ oz butter
20 ml/¾ fl. oz brandy or madeira
6 to 8 sheets gelatine
300 gr/11 oz Waldorf salad (see p. 134)
100 gr/3½ oz meat aspic
some mandarin segments and pistachios for garnishing

Time Necessary:

Pre-heat the oven to 220°C/425°F
Preparation: 1 hr 40 min (without cooling time)
Service: 15 minutes

 Advice

This dish can be extended using venison ham. Saddle of venison goes very well with orange sauce or Cumberland sauce.

Preparation:

1. Prepare the saddle of venison for roasting. Remove any skin with a sharp knife.
2. Stick some wire skewers through the backbone so that while cooking the flesh does not go out of shape. Season the saddle with salt and pepper and fry off the meat side in a frying pan.
3. Roast the saddle in an oven heated to 220°C/425°F until cooked. This should take about 20 minutes. Take the saddle immediately from the pan and allow it to get cold. Finally remove the skewers.
4. While cooking, prepare the garnish. Peel and halve the pears, so that each half has some stalk attached to it. Remove the core section using a pommes parisienne cutter.
5. Blanch the pear halves in syrup to which has been added some white wine and lemon juice, then allow the liquor to get cold.
6. While the pears are blanching, clean and wash the chanterelles. Peel and chop an onion finely, then sweat off chanterelles and onion in a pan together with oil, salt and pepper.
7. Drain the pear halves, garnish with a leaf of lamb's lettuce, and fill the cavity with the chanterelle and onion mixture.
8. Cut off the stalks from the figs and free all the fruit from the skins with the aid of a teaspoon.
9. Beat the calves' liver sausage with the butter to a smooth paste and flavour with madeira or brandy.
10. Now prepare the saddle for service. Remove the meat from the backbone.
11. Soften the gelatine in cold water, drain off and lightly warm it until it has dissolved. Now mix the gelatine with the Waldorf salad. The gelatine must not be too cold, or lumps will be formed.
12. Using the Waldorf salad, rebuild the shape of the saddle as it was.
13. Placing both fillets together, cut them into 5 mm/¼" slices at a slight angle.
14. Beginning at the back, pass each slice through almost cold aspic and then lay them onto the rebuilt saddle, overlapping them as you go. In order to keep them in place, use toothpicks. Any unused slices will be used to decorate the dish.
15. Leave the prepared saddle in a cool place to set, then remove the wire skewers.
16. Using a star tube, pipe a line of liver mousse along the centre of the saddle, and garnish this with the mandarin segments and pistachio nuts.

The fillets are only removed when the saddle is completely cold

The original shape of the saddle is built up again with the Waldorf salad

The slices are laid on the Waldorf salad from the end with the ribs

Service:

17. Set the saddle of venison in the left upper corner of the serving dish.
18. Place the figs parallel to the saddle on the right-hand side.
19. The stuffed pears are placed in a line running from below the saddle to the top right-hand corner.

20. Any remaining slices of the fillets are placed fanwise in the spaces left in the top and bottom corners.

Herb-Coated Venison Fillet with Stewed Autumn Vegetables

To serve 8:

1800 gr/4 lbs saddle of venison (middle)

salt, pepper

oil for frying

1 bunch parsley

1 bunch chives

1 bunch samphire

1 bunch borage

1 bunch chervil

100 gr/3½ oz lean veal

100 gr/3½ oz cream

300 gr/11 oz pig's caul

8 beetroots

400 gr/14 oz Brussels sprouts

600 gr/21 oz salsify

sugar, vinegar

Cumberland sauce (see p. 173)

Time Necessary:

Pre-heat the oven to 200°C/400°F
Preparation time: 120 minutes (without cooling time)
Service: 10 minutes

Preparation:

1. Trim all sinews and fat from the saddle of venison. Remove the two loin fillets.
2. Remove the fillets (undercut) from the saddle.
3. Scrape the ends of the rib bones, and roast the carcase in an oven heated to 200°C/400°F for about 15 minutes, then allow to cool.
4. Clean, wash and chop the herbs finely.
5. Cut up the undercut fillets and the veal finely and with the addition of the cream, pass the whole through a food processor or liquidiser. Season with salt and pepper.
6. Add the finely chopped herbs to the purée and season again, if necessary.
7. Soften the pig's caul in water, then allow to drain. Spread it out and cut into two.
8. Spread the prepared stuffing onto the pig's caul, then lay on each piece one of the loin fillets seasoned with salt and pepper, and wrap them up.
9. Lay the loin fillets on an oiled baking sheet and cook in an oven heated to 200°C/400°F for about 20 minutes. Then take them out of the oven and allow them to cool.
10. For the garnish, wash the beetroots and cook them in salted water with a dash of vinegar for about 30 minutes.
11. Take them out of the water, allow them to cool, then remove the skins.
12. Cut the bottoms level, then cut off one third from their height, hollow out the bases and put them to one side.
13. Clean and blanch the Brussels sprouts.
14. Wash and peel the salsify, then wash again and blanch.
15. Heat the sugar until it caramelises, deglaze with vinegar and top up the pan with water. Cook out well, seasoning with salt and pepper.
16. Place the salsify and the Brussels sprouts into the marinade.
17. Drain off the vegetables, then fill them into the beetroot bases.

Service:

18. Cut both loin fillets into the same sized slices.
19. Place the carcase diagonally into the top left corner of the serving dish. Lay a row of the loin slices on the left side of the carcase running down to the bottom edge, then follow up with another row on the right side, in an arc to the top right corner, each slice slightly overlapping the other.
20. Arrange 5 beet halves below the saddle and 3 above or between the two arcs. Serve the Cumberland sauce separately in a sauceboat.

Before you can bone the loin fillets, any sinews and fat must be removed

The undercut fillets are removed with a sharp knife

The loin fillet is laid on to the herb stuffing covered with pig's caul

119

Calves' Liver Parfait with Frisée (Curly Endive) Salad

To serve 8:

200 gr/7 oz Calves' liver	
30 gr/1 oz flour	
4 eggs	
150 ml/5¼ fl. oz milk	
50 gr/1¾ oz cream	
salt, pepper, nutmeg	
1 large pinch of garlic granules	
20 ml/¾ fl. oz brandy	
100 ml/3½ fl. oz meat aspic	
1 frisée salad (curly endive)	
vinegar, oil	

Time Necessary:

Prepare the previous day
Preparation: 1 hr 20 min
(without cooling time)
Service: 15 minutes

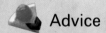 Advice

If the terrine is made the previous day it can be left overnight to cool. Serve it with brioche-type bread.

Preparation:

1. Cut the calves' liver small and pass through a food processor or liquidiser into a fine purée.
2. Sieve the flour and add it to the purée. Separate two eggs, and beat in the yolks, together with the remaining eggs to the mixture, then mix in the milk.
3. Beat the cream stiff, then fold this into the mixture.
4. Season well with salt, pepper, nutmeg, garlic granules and brandy.
5. Fill into an oval terrine mould and close with aluminium foil.
6. Cook at 180°C/350°F in a water-bath in the oven for about 1 hour. Check if cooked with a needle.
7. Allow the terrine to get cold, then pour over the meat aspic.

Service:

8. Clean and wash the frisée salad, before dressing it with salt, pepper, oil and vinegar.
9. Arrange the terrine to one side of a round dish, placing the dressed frisée salad at the side.
10. Using a warmed dessertspoon, take out some of the parfait, and arrange this on top of the frisée salad.

Poultry Liver Parfait with Green Peppers

To serve 8:

400 gr/14 oz poultry livers
(chicken or turkey etc)

200 ml/9 fl. oz white wine

1 dessertspoon port

1 teaspoon ground paprika

150 gr/5¼ oz cold butter

salt, white milled pepper

1 dessertspoon green
peppercorns

100 gr/3½ oz meat aspic

1 frisée salad (curly endive)

vinegar, oil

Time Necessary:

Preparation: 35 minutes
(without cooling time)
Service: 10 minutes

Advice

Calves' liver may be used instead
of poultry livers for this dish.

Preparation:

1. Remove all sinews and fat from the livers.
2. Heat the white wine without letting it boil and soak the livers in it for 3 minutes. Pour off the liquid and allow the livers to cool.
3. Then purée the livers in a food processor or liquidiser. Add the port and the paprika, then beat in the cold butter. Season with salt and pepper, and put in the green peppercorns.
4. Put the mixture into an oval terrine mould.
5. Allow to cool in the refrigerator, and then pour over the almost-cold meat aspic.

Service:

6. Clean and wash the frisée salad, before dressing it with salt, pepper, oil and vinegar.
7. Arrange the terrine to one side of a round dish, placing the dressed frisée salad at the side.
8. Using a warmed dessertspoon, take out some of the parfait, and arrange this on top of the frisée salad.

Terrine of Calves' Sweetbreads with Chervil Sauce

To serve 8:

600 gr/21 oz calves' sweetbreads

salt, pepper

1 onion

2 cloves

1 bayleaf

200 gr/7 oz fresh leaf spinach

1 shallot

2 dessertspoons oil

nutmeg

1 clove garlic

4 eggs

200 gr/7 oz cream

1 oakleaf lettuce

vinegar, oil

150 gr/5¼ oz Parma ham

chervil sauce (see p. 171)

Time Necessary:

Preparation: 1 hr 30 min
(without cooling time)
Service: 15 minutes

Advice

Lambs' sweetbreads may also be used for this recipe.

Preparation:

1. Rinse the sweetbreads several times in fresh cold water, then remove all traces of coarse skin and fat.
2. Now season them with salt and pepper, and roll them into suitable clingfilm. Close the ends of the clingfilm well.
3. Peel the onion, stick it with the cloves and place with the bayleaf in a pan of lightly salted water. Bring the pan to the boil, place in the sweetbreads and cook for 8 minutes, allowing them to get cold in the cooking water.
4. Look over the spinach leaves. Remove the stalks and then wash the leaves well. Then blanch briefly in salted water.
5. Peel the shallots and chop them finely. Heat the oil in a pan and sweat off the shallots, add the spinach, then season with salt, pepper, nutmeg and a little garlic. Finally allow to cool.
6. While cooking, line a loaf tin with suitable clingfilm.
7. Beat the eggs with the cream. Season with salt, pepper, and a little nutmeg. Mix in the prepared spinach mixture.
8. Unwrap the sweetbreads and remove any further skin and fat, if necessary.
9. Half-fill the loaf tin with the spinach and egg mixture, then lay the sweetbreads on top, finally filling the tin with the rest of the spinach and egg mixture. Press down lightly to remove any air bubbles.
10. Seal the terrine with suitable clingfilm and cook in a water-bath in the oven, heated to 150°C/300°F, for 45 minutes, taking care that the temperature of the water-bath does not exceed 80°C/175°F. Test if cooked with a needle. Take the terrine out of the water-bath and allow to cool.

Service:

11. When the terrine is completely cold, wash and clean the salad. Dress it with salt, pepper, oil and vinegar. Lay it out at the edge of a round dish.
12. Turn out the terrine and cut it into 15 mm/¾" slices. Arrange the slices around the dish on the salad, slightly overlapping one another.
13. Arrange a rose from the Parma ham in the centre of the dish.
14. Serve the chervil sauce separately in a sauceboat or bowl.

Remove all fat and skin from the sweetbreads

The sweetbreads are rolled into the clingfilm and the ends sealed

The sweetbreads form the centre layer of the terrine

VEGETABLES
AND SALADS

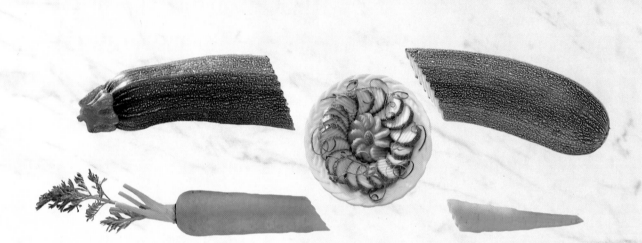

Green and White Asparagus with Black Forest Ham

Preparation:

1. Prepare the asparagus for cooking. The white asparagus should be peeled evenly from tip to end. Cut off about 1 cm/$\frac{1}{2}$″ from the ends, then tie with twine into bundles each of 200 gr/7 oz.
2. Place the asparagus into plenty of boiling water to which has been added the butter, sugar and salt, and cook for about 12 minutes. Allow to cool in the liquor.
3. Green asparagus is not, as a rule, peeled. Only the upper part is used and the woody lower parts of the stalks are cut off. Cut all the sticks to the same length.
4. Cook the tips in boiling salted water. The cooking time will depend on the thickness of the stalks, and will be about 5 to 7 minutes. Refresh the green asparagus after cooking in cold water.

Service:

5. Allow the cooked white asparagus to drain thoroughly. Cut off the ends obliquely, and cut the stalks in half at the same angle.
6. First arrange the white asparagus tips in a circle with the ends pointing outwards. Follow this by laying the green asparagus tips on top in the same fashion, finishing with the bottom halves of the white asparagus stalks.
7. Form the slices of ham into rosettes and arrange them in the centre. Garnish with a few salad leaves and chive stalks.
8. Serve the dish with egg and herb dressing.

To serve 8:

2000 gr/4$\frac{1}{2}$ lbs white asparagus

juice of 2 lemons

100 gr/3$\frac{1}{2}$ oz butter

salt, sugar

1000 gr/2$\frac{1}{4}$ lbs green asparagus

700 gr/1$\frac{1}{2}$ lbs Black Forest ham

a few salad leaves and some chopped chives for garnishing

egg and herb dressing (see p. 172)

Time Necessary:

Preparation: 1 hr 10 min (without cooling time)
Service: 20 minutes

Advice

The asparagus cuttings may be kept and used to make a cream of asparagus soup.

Terrine of Chanterelle Mushrooms with Smoked Leg of Lamb

To serve 8:

6 sheets gelatine
1 bunch parsley
400 gr/14 oz fresh chanterelle mushrooms
1 onion
2 carrots
oil
250 ml/9 fl. oz meat stock
salt, pepper
400 gr/14 oz sliced smoked leg of lamb

Time Necessary:

Prepare the previous day
Preparation: 60 minutes
(without cooling time)
Service: 15 minutes

Preparation:

1. Soak the sheet gelatine in cold water. Pluck the parsley from the stalks, wash and chop finely.
2. Wash and peel the chanterelles. Peel the onion and cut into fine dice.
3. Wash and peel the carrots, cut into fine dice and blanch briefly in salted boiling water, leaving them crisp.
4. Heat the oil in a pan, add the onion and chanterelles, then sweat off lightly. Add the stock and bring to the boil.
5. Add the carrots and the chopped parsley, together with the drained gelatine. Season with salt and pepper.
6. Fill into a terrine mould and place in the refrigerator for at least 12 hours.

Service:

7. On the next day, place the mould momentarily into hot water, then turn out and cut into 8 even slices, using a hot knife.
8. Arrange the slices at the top of a serving dish at an angle and overlapping, with any extra slices below.
9. Fold the slices of smoked lamb and lay them to right and left of the slices of terrine.

 Advice

Serve a chive and yoghurt sauce with this dish.

Vegetable Dish with Basil and Olive Oil Vinaigrette Dressing

To serve 8 to 10:

250 gr/9 oz mange-tout (sugar peas/snow peas)

2 courgettes (zucchini)

4 carrots

3 kohlrabi

1 bunch radishes

1 bunch basil

100 ml/3½ fl. oz olive oil

5 dessertspoons sherry vinegar

salt, pepper

some type of curly salad leaf e.g. curly-endive (frisée)

Time Necessary:

Preparation: 40 minutes
Service: 15 minutes

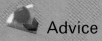 **Advice**

This dish makes a good supplement to all roast meat dishes.

Preparation:

1. Clean the mange-tout, blanch briefly to retain crispness and drain well.
2. Then wash the courgettes (zucchini), cutting into slices with a corrugated decorating knife, and blanching them in the same way.
3. Peel the carrots, and cut them like the courgettes and blanch.
4. Peel the kohlrabi, cut in halves lengthwise, cut them into slices and blanch.
5. Wash the radishes, remove the green tops and slice, but not too thinly.
6. Wash the basil, pull off the stalks, and chop the leaves finely.
7. Mix the olive oil and vinegar together, season with salt and pepper, and add the basil to the mixture.

Service:

8. Take a round dish, preferably one with a slightly raised edge. Cover the base of the plates with some of the dressing.
9. Working from the outside towards the centre, arrange the mange-tout all round the dish, overlapping each one. Follow with the other vegetables, in turn, to give a colour contrast.

10. Finish off the centre of the dish with a small garnish of curly-endive (frisée).
11. Brush the remaining marinade carefully over the vegetables.

Mushroom Salad

To serve 8:

800 gr/28 oz button mushrooms

2 shallots

1 small clove garlic

5 dessertspoons oil for frying

juice of 2 lemons

1 bunch chives

salt, pepper

vinegar, oil

Time Necessary:

Preparation: 25 minutes

Preparation:

1. Wash, clean and quarter the mushrooms.
2. Peel the shallots and chop finely. Peel the garlic and chop finely.
3. Heat the oil in a large pan and sweat off the shallot and garlic together.
4. Put in the mushrooms and moisten with the lemon juice. Salt lightly. Stew a little and remove from the liquor.
5. Reduce the liquor to one half, then put back the mushrooms.
6. Wash and finely chop the chives. Add to the mushrooms and season the salad with salt, pepper, vinegar and oil.

Vegetable Salad

To serve 8:

1 celeriac (about 300 gr/11 oz)	
3 carrots	
1 courgette (zucchini)	
1 red capsicum	
1 green capsicum	
salt, pepper	
vinegar, oil	
1 bunch parsley	

Time Necessary:

Preparation: 25 minutes

Preparation:

1. Wash and peel the celeriac, then cut it into 5 mm/$\frac{1}{4}$" dice. Peel the carrots and cut them into the same size dice.
2. Blanch the carrot and celeriac, plunge briefly in boiling salted water, then drain well.
3. Wash, clean, peel and dice the courgettes (Zucchini). Wash the capsicum, cut into halves, remove seeds, then cut into the same size dice as the other vegetables.
4. Mix all the ingredients together in a large bowl, season with salt, and dress with vinegar and oil. Allow to stand for about 1 hour.
5. Wash the parsley, pull off the stalks, and chop the leaves finely. Mix some of the parsley into the salad, and sprinkle the rest over the salad before serving.

Advice

To serve this dish lay out some salad leaves and place the vegetable salad on top.

Waldorf Salad

To serve 8:

juice of 1 lemon

1 celeriac (350 gr/12½ oz)

5 apples (Granny Smith, or other crisp, juicy apple)

200 gr/7 oz mayonnaise

125 gr/4 oz sour cream

100 gr/3½ oz whipping cream

salt, pepper, sugar

garnish with some walnut kernels and mandarin segments

Time Necessary:

Preparation: 35 minutes

Preparation:

1. Mix the lemon juice with some water.
2. Wash and peel the celeriac. Cut first into thin slices, then cut into 3 cm/1¼″ strips.
3. Wash, peel and core the apples, then cut into slices before cutting also into strips.
4. Place the prepared apple and celeriac strips into the waiting lemon water, swirl around, then remove and drain off well.
5. Mix the mayonnaise well with the sour cream, then mix in with the apple and celeriac strips. Season with salt, pepper, and a little sugar.
6. Beat the cream until stiff, then fold into the salad.
7. Put the salad into a glass bowl and garnish with walnut kernels and mandarin segments.

CHEESE,
BREAD
AND FRUIT

Cheese Salad with Ham and Salami Strips

To serve 8:

500 gr/18 oz Emmental cheese

200 gr/7 oz cooked sliced ham

100 gr/3½ oz sliced salami

2 carrots

2 hard-boiled eggs

1 lettuce

vinegar, salt, pepper, oil

Time Necessary:

Preparation: 25 minutes
Marination: 2 hours
Service: 5 minutes

Preparation:

1. Wash and peel the carrots, and cut into dice. Blanch briefly.
2. Cut the Emmental cheese into strips and separate.
3. Cut the ham and salami into similar strips.
4. Mix all the ingredients together in a bowl.
5. Season the salad with salt, pepper, vinegar and oil, then leave to stand for 2 hours.

Service:

6. Clean the lettuce well, wash and drain, then line a bowl with the leaves, before putting in the cheese salad.
7. Cut the hard-boiled eggs into 6 and garnish the salad with the segments.

Chive Cream Cheese with Steamed Potatoes and Cherry Tomatoes

To serve 8:

2 bunches chives

750 gr/26½ oz quark (soft curd cheese made from skimmed milk)

100 gr/3½ oz cream

salt, pepper

1 lettuce for garnish

200 gr/7 oz cherry tomatoes

1000 gr/35 oz small new potatoes

1 teaspoon caraway seeds

Time Necessary:

Preparation: 35 minutes

Preparation:

1. Wash the chives and chop finely.
2. Beat the quark together with the cream to a smooth paste. Add the chopped chives, and season with salt and pepper.
3. Clean and wash the lettuce, then line a glass bowl with it.
4. Fill the cream and cheese mixture into the bowl, smooth off the top, and make a pattern on it with a toothed pastry scraper.
5. Remove the stalks from the cherry tomatoes and wash them. Arrange them around the edge of the glass bowl.
6. Boil the potatoes in salted water for 20 minutes with the caraway seeds. Pour off the water, then peel half of the potatoes.
7. Put the potatoes into a bowl, and serve them with the chive cream cheese.

 Advice

Keep the potatoes warm on a heated hot-plate (réchaud).

139

Mozzarella Cheese with Basil and Tomatoes

To serve 6:

4 beef tomatoes

800 gr/28 oz mozzarella cheese

1 bunch basil

salt, pepper

2 dessertspoons oil

Time Necessary:

Preparation: 5 minutes
Service: 15 minutes

Preparation:

1. Wash and stalk the beef tomatoes, then cut into slices.
2. Cut the mozzarella cheese also into slices.

Service:

3. Alternate the cheese and tomato slices around the edge of a round plate, then continue with a second row, overlapping the slices all the time.
4. Wash the basil, retain a couple of leaves for garnishing, then chop the rest finely, and sprinkle over the cheese.
5. Shortly before serving, season the cheese and tomato slices with salt and pepper and sprinkle the oil over the top. Garnish with the remaining basil leaves.

Pickled Sheep's Milk Cheese with Thyme and Rosemary

Pickle beforehand for
4 weeks
Preparation: 20 minutes
Marination: 4 weeks
Service: 5 minutes

To serve 8:

800 gr/28 oz sheep's milk cheese

2 cloves garlic

4 shallots

1 sprig thyme

1 sprig rosemary

1 bayleaf

8 white peppercorns

500 ml/18 fl. oz oil

250 ml/9 fl. oz olive oil

1 lollo rosso lettuce

1 bunch chives

Time Necessary:

Preparation:

1. Cut the sheep's milk cheese into slices and lay them into a glass mould.
2. Peel the clove of garlic and halve lengthwise. Peel the shallots and cut into three. Break up the thyme and rosemary into three.
3. Sprinkle the shallots, garlic, bayleaf, thyme, rosemary and peppercorns over the cheese. Finally fill up with both kinds of oil.
4. Seal the mould airtight, and leave the cheese for about 4 weeks to marinate.

Service:

5. Clean and wash the lollo rosso lettuce. Line the edge of a glass dish with it. Lay the cheese slices in the dish. Pour over the marinade, together with the pickling herbs and spices.
6. Wash the chives, then chop finely before sprinkling over the cheese slices.

141

Italian Cheeses with Celery Sticks

To serve 6:

1 head celery
400 gr/14 oz black grapes
200 gr/7 oz Gorgonzola in the piece
200 gr/7 oz Parmesan in the piece
200 gr/7 oz Provolone in the piece
200 gr/7 oz Robiola in the piece

Time Necessary:

Preparation: 10 minutes
Service: 10 minutes

 Advice

● Cheese should be served on an unvarnished wooden board, at room temperature.
● A round board fitted with a turntable is very useful as it allows easy cutting of the different cheeses.
● Apart from a garnish, e.g. grapes and nuts, serve a selection of different breads and butter.

Preparation:

1. Cut the celery sticks from the root and remove the coarse strings from the sticks with a potato peeler. Clean up the stalks, then wash and drain well.
2. Arrange the prepared celery in a celery glass or glass vase with fresh cold water.
3. Wash the grapes and allow to drain off completely.

Service:

4. Begin with the gorgonzola in the top right corner of the dish. Leave the cheese in the piece.
5. Arrange the Parmesan cheese in the left upper part of the dish. To cut the Parmesan either a special knife, or a sharp table knife may be used.
6. Cut the Provolone and Robiola into slices.
7. Lay the Provolone below the gorgonzola overlapping the slices, following the shape of the dish.
8. Now lay out the Robiola in the same way, below the Parmesan.

9. Stand the celery glass in the centre at the top of the dish and arrange the bunch of grapes in the centre of the dish.

French Cheese Selection with Grapes and Radishes

To serve 8:

2 bunches radishes

150 gr/5$\frac{1}{4}$ oz Brie

150 gr/5$\frac{1}{4}$ oz Camembert

150 gr/5$\frac{1}{4}$ oz sheep's milk cheese

150 gr/5$\frac{1}{4}$ oz goat's cheese

200 gr/7 oz Reblochon

200 gr/7 oz blue cheese (Roquefort)

600 gr/21 oz black grapes

Time Necessary:

Preparation: 30 minutes
Service: 5 minutes

 Advice

Soft cheese types are not cut in order to stop them running. Cheeses are not served too cold, as their flavours are best appreciated at room temperature. Table knives are used for cutting—usually one for each type of cheese.

Preparation:

1. Wash the radishes thoroughly. Remove leaves and roots. Using a sharp knife, roses, buds, flowers or daisies can be made. Allow the radishes to stand for 30 minutes in cold water after cutting. For roses 5 cuts are needed around the radish, then 5 smaller cuts between the others. Cut the root area off completely flat in a circle. For flowers, the radish is cut about 3 mm/$\frac{1}{8}$" from the centre from top to bottom.
For buds the radish is cut across four times in one direction and six times in the other.
For daisies, twelve cuts are made in the radish from the stalk end almost down to the root. Cut the "petals" free using the point of the knife, so that the white inside parts shown when open.
It is much quicker to use a special radish flower cutter. These will give a more uniform effect to the finished product.

Service:

2. Arrange the cheeses clockwise around the board, beginning with the mildest cheese and continuing around with the remaining cheeses according to their taste.
3. Wash the grapes, and dry well. Arrange the grapes and radishes in the centre of the board, garnishing with vine leaves, if desired.

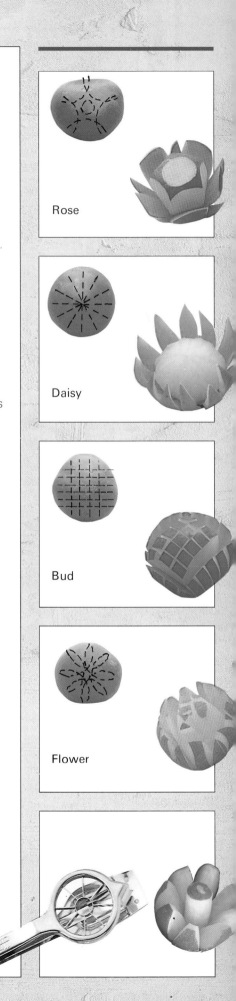

Rose

Daisy

Bud

Flower

Blue Cheese Selection with Walnuts

To serve 6:

1 stick celery

300 gr/11 oz Blue Stilton cheese

300 gr/11 oz Gorgonzola cheese

300 gr/11 oz Roquefort cheese

130 gr/4 oz walnut kernels

40 ml/1½ fl. oz port

Time Necessary:

Preparation: 10 minutes
Decoration: 10 minutes

Advice

Stilton can be eaten by taking a little from the centre of the cheese and spreading it on a piece of bread. The mild flavour of the port harmonises well with the full aroma of the cheese.

Preparation:

1. Cut the root from the celery and remove the strings from the outer stalks. Clean well under running water, scrubbing if necessary. Dry the celery sticks well.
2. Make a hollow in the top of the Stilton cheese with a dessertspoon.

Service:

3. Place the Gorgonzola into the right upper part of the dish, with the Roquefort to the left. The Stilton is then placed at the bottom in the centre.

4. Cut the celery sticks across diagonally and pull off the leaves.
5. Arrange the lower part of the celery sticks from the centre pointing out towards the edge of the dish.
6. Lay some leaves on top of the sticks of celery.
7. Put the walnut kernels in a glass dish between the Gorgonzola and the Roquefort, on the cheese platter.
8. Pour the port into the hollowed-out Stilton.

Advice

● If possible, cheese should always be stored away from other foodstuffs, and each type of cheese should be kept wrapped separately in greaseproof paper (parchment paper).
● When buying soft cheeses the degree of maturity should always be checked at the time of purchase, either visually in the case of cut cheeses, or by finger pressure in the case of small whole cheeses. Cheese should be evenly ripe throughout. A strong smell of ammonia denotes a cheese which is past its best.
● In a selection of cheeses there should always be variety of colour and type, such as a blue cheese, a soft cheese, a semi-hard cheese and a hard cheese.
● Cheese is often arranged on a round wooden board clockwise, with cheeses arranged in a circle starting with the mildest and finishing with the strongest.

Cheese Dish with Salted Sticks

To serve 8:

200 gr/7 oz sliced Edam
200 gr/7 oz sliced Emmental
200 gr/7 oz sliced Tilsit
200 gr/7 oz Camembert
200 gr/7 oz Brie
200 gr/7 oz Bavarian Blue
1 pack salted sticks
1 bunch radishes, prepared as described on p. 144
some leaves of frisée lettuce

Time Necessary:

Service: 15 minutes

Preparation:

1. Arrange the sliced cheeses around the edge of the dish in a semicircle. Begin on the outside with the Emmental, lightly overlapping the slices.
2. Follow up with the Tilsit and Edam cheeses.

3. Cut the Camembert into 8 even segments and arrange them in a circle, points inwards, in the bottom left-hand corner of the dish.
4. Place the section of Brie above the Camembert with the point towards the centre of the dish.
5. Cut 4 slices from the Bavarian Blue, leaving the rest of the piece whole. Arrange this cheese in the top left-hand corner, with the slices fanned out below, lightly overlapping.

6. Arrange the salted sticks in the centre of the dish, in a pile, with the salad leaves and radishes as decoration.

Puff Pastry Pockets with Creamed Cheese

To serve 8:

500 gr/18 oz puff pastry (frozen commercial product)	
150 gr/5¼ oz Roquefort	
200 gr/7 oz butter	
150 gr/5¼ oz Camembert	
salt, pepper	
1 teaspoon ground paprika	
1 dessertspoon chopped parsley	
2 eggyolks	
some poppy (maw) seeds	
some sesame seeds	
some caraway seeds	

Time Necessary:

Pre-heat the oven to
220°C/425°F
Preparation: 40 minutes
Resting time: 45 minutes
Service: 5 minutes

Preparation:

1. Allow the pastry to thaw.
2. Pass the Roquefort through a hair sieve and mix to a smooth cream with 100 gr/3½ oz butter.
3. Repeat the above process separately with the Camembert.
4. Halve the Camembert mixture, season half with salt, pepper and paprika, and the other half with parsley, salt and pepper.
5. Because of its strong flavour, the Roquefort cream should not be further seasoned.
6. Roll out the puff pastry evenly to a thickness of 5 mm/¼".
7. Cut out the pastry into circles, using a fluted round cutter of 3 cm/1¼" diameter.
8. Beat the eggyolks with a little water and paint it on the circles, before laying them on to a baking sheet (sheet pan). Coat a third of the circles each with the poppy, sesame and caraway seeds.
9. Allow the pastry circles to rest for 45 minutes. It is important to allow this time in order that they rise evenly during baking.
10. Bake off for 5 minutes in an oven heated to 220°C/425°F.
11. After baking allow to cool before cutting each puff across in the centre.
12. Pipe the prepared cheese creams into the halves of the puffs, using a star tube, then put a lid on each.

Service:

13. Arrange the cheese pockets in rows on a serving dish.

Advice

The puff pastry trimmings can be used to make cheese straws. Put all the trimmings together flat and press lightly, without kneading. Roll out anew. Cut the pastry into 1 cm/½" strips and sprinkle these with paprika and grated cheese. Twist the strips and lay them on to a baking sheet (sheet pan) and bake in the same way as for the recipe. When cool cut into 5 cm/2" lengths.

Cheese Pastries

Preparation:

1. Cream the butter well and add the grated cheese.
2. Mix in the flour and baking powder, adding the cream little by little. Season with salt and pepper.
3. Allow the dough to stand for about two hours in a cool place.
4. Roll out the dough evenly to 5 mm/$\frac{1}{4}$'' thickness and cut out into various shapes, using either a knife or pastry cutters.
5. Knead the remaining pastry together and leave in a cool place.
6. Beat the eggyolks with a little water and paint the cut out pastry with it, then sprinkle the cut out pastry shapes with the caraway seeds, poppy seeds, sesame seeds and coarse salt, as desired, keeping one type of topping to each shape.
7. Bake the shapes in an oven heated to 230°C/450°F for 5 minutes, then take out and allow to cool.
8. Form the left-over pastry into a roll about 4 cm/1$\frac{1}{2}$'' in diameter and cut this into slices about 5 mm/$\frac{1}{4}$'' thick. Bake off these discs in the same way as the others for 5 minutes.

Service:

9. Cover a serving dish with a dish paper or a doyley and arrange the pastries in rows, according to shape.

To serve 8:

200 gr/7 oz butter
200 gr/7 oz grated cheese
375 gr/13 oz flour
1 teaspoon baking powder
100 gr/3$\frac{1}{2}$ oz cream
salt, pepper
2 eggyolks
caraway, poppy (maw), and sesame seeds for sprinkling on top

Time Necessary:

Pre-heat the oven to 230°C/450°F
Preparation: 30 minutes
Resting time: 2 hours
Service: 5 minutes

Italian Olive Oil Flat Bread

To serve 8 to 10:

70 gr/2½ oz yeast

about 300 ml/11 fl. oz water

1000 gr/35 oz wheat flour

1 dessertspoon salt

5 dessertspoons olive oil

Time Necessary:

Pre-heat the oven to
250°C/480°F
Preparation: 40 minutes
Resting time: 4 hours

Preparation:

1. Dissolve the yeast in 100 ml/3½ fl. oz lukewarm water
   and work in a little flour.
2. Leave this paste in a warm place to work for about 10
   minutes.
3. Flatten out this paste lightly on to a floured work surface
   and add the rest of the flour, salt and water. Knead
   together thoroughly.
4. Beat the dough on to the work surface many times, then
   allow to stand for about 4 hours, to prove.
5. Roll out the dough into circles about 1 cm/½″ thick and
   place them on an oiled and salted baking sheet (sheet
   pan).
6. Press dents into the dough with the fingers at intervals
   of about 5 cm/2″ and sprinkle olive oil on to the top of
   the dough, and a light dusting of salt.
7. Bake the bread until light brown, in an oven heated to
   250°C/480°F. If the top heat is too great, cover the bread
   with aluminium foil to prevent burning.

Bread Basket of Mixed-Grain, Wholemeal and White Bread

To serve 8 to 10:

2 French sticks

1 small wholemeal loaf

1 party-round (see note on the
right)

1 small mixed grain loaf

8 poppy seed crescent rolls

Time Necessary:

Service: 10 minutes

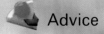 **Advice**

If it is to be obtained
commercially, order the party-
round from your supplier giving
a couple of days notice.

Service:

1. Cut 1 French stick diagonally into 4 pieces,
   the other into slices.
2. Cut the mixed-grain and wholemeal bread in
   the same way.
3. Line a bread basket with a serviette. Place the
   party-round* on the right and the white bread
   pieces beside it, at an angle. Arrange the mixed-
   grain, wholemeal and white bread slices to the
   left, fanwise. Fill the remaining space with the
   poppy seed rolls.

*A party-round is a round of
bread rolls baked together so
that they are lightly joined,
and each one is decorated
with a different type of seed,
the whole being decorated
with dough shapes.
(see illustration)

Bread Basket of Bread Sticks and Salted Breads

Service:

1. Line a flat bread basket with a serviette.
2. Cut the bread sticks diagonally in half and arrange one of each of them in the basket with the cut ends pointing outwards.
3. Cut the other half into slices.
4. Arrange the bread slices into four rows in a half circle, following the shape of the basket. Begin at the outside with the rye bread, following with the white and then the nut bread.
5. On the left-hand side lay the salted pretzels and the salted rolls on the right.

To serve 8:

1 French stick

1 nut bread stick

1 rye bread stick

8 small salted pretzels

8 small salted rolls

Time Necessary:

Service: 10 minutes

 Advice

If buying the salted goods commercially give a couple of days notice to your supplier.

Exotic Fruit Platter with Maraschino

How the orange segments are cut

To serve 8:

150 gr/5¼ oz sugar

150 ml/5¼ fl. oz water

juice of 2 lemons

40 ml/1½ fl. oz maraschino

1 mango

2 oranges

3 kiwifruit

4 fresh figs

1 papaya (pawpaw)

2 bananas

Time Necessary:

Preparation: 30 minutes
Decoration: 15 minutes

Preparation:

1. Cook the sugar in the water to produce a clear syrup. Allow to cool, then add the lemon juice and maraschino.
2. Prepare the various fruits. Peel the mango and cut into segments from the stone.
3. Peel the oranges to the flesh and cut into segments, adding any juice produced to the syrup.
4. Peel the kiwifruit and slice thinly.
5. Cut the bottoms from the figs and remove the flesh whole with the aid of a teaspoon. Cut into halves lengthwise.
6. Halve the pawpaws remove the pips with a spoon then cut each half into segments, removing the skin.
7. Peel the bananas and cut into diagonal slices.

Service:

8. Arrange the fruits fan-wise on a round dish, beginning with the mangoes, then the kiwifruit, the oranges, pawpaws and finally the banana slices. The halved figs are placed in the centre.

9. Glaze the fruits with the syrup, using a brush.

The figs are removed whole from the skins, with a teaspoon

Pears Filled with Dark Chocolate Mousse

To serve 8:

juice of 2 lemons

50 gr/1¾ oz sugar

100 ml/3½ fl. oz white wine

200 ml/7 fl. oz water

4 pears

For the mousse:

4 egg yolks

1 teaspoon icing (confectioner's) sugar

20 ml/¾ fl. oz kirschwasser brandy

1 teaspoon soluble coffee powder

3 dessertspoons water

175 gr/6 oz plain dessert chocolate

125 gr/4 oz butter

4 egg whites

some salt

For the garnish:

orange segments, cocktail cherries, or small ice wafers

Time Necessary:

Preparation: 20 minutes (without cooling time)
Service: 10 minutes

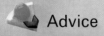 Advice

In place of pears, other fruit or different flavoured mousses may be used.

Preparation:

1. Put the lemon juice, sugar, white wine, and water into a pan and bring it to the boil.
2. Wash the pears and cut through the centre, leaving some of the stalk on each half.
3. Remove the seed housing and core with a pommes parisienne cutter (ball cutter).
4. Lay the pear halves into the liquor, bring to the boil once and leave to cool in the liquor.
5. Prepare the mousse. Beat the icing sugar and eggyolks until frothy.
6. Add the kirschwasser and beat over a water bath for about 10 minutes until hot and frothy. Beat again when cold.
7. Dissolve the coffee powder in hot water, and then melt the chocolate in it.
8. Beat the butter to a cream and add the chocolate and coffee mixture to it.
9. Add the butter mixture to the cold egg yolk mixture.
10. Beat the egg whites with a little salt until stiff.
11. Take about an eighth of the egg white mixture and beat this into the chocolate and egg yolk mixture, then beat in the rest of the egg white mixture.
12. Fill the mousse into a bowl and leave in a cold place for about 5 hours to set.

Service:

13. Dry the pear halves and cut a little from the outside curve, so they will stand level.
14. Fill the mousse into a piping bag fitted with a star tube, and pipe it into the pear halves.
15. Decorate the pear halves with orange segments, cocktail cherries or wafers, and arrange on a round plate or dish, with the stalks pointing inwards.

Fruit Salad in Pineapple

To serve 8:

4 small pineapples

4 oranges

2 apples

2 pears

2 bananas

200 gr/7 oz black grapes

juice of 1 lemon

40 ml/1½ fl. oz maraschino

some sugar

Time Necessary:

Preparation: 15 minutes
Allow fruit to stand for 1 hour
Service: 10 minutes

Preparation:

1. Cut the top leaves from the pineapples with scissors.
2. Halve the pineapples lengthwise, then hollow out the fruit from the pineapples to about 1 cm/½" from the edge of the skin.
3. Cut the pineapple shells obliquely from the root to the centre, so that they will stand at an angle.
4. Cut the removed fruit flesh into 1 cm/½" thick slices and remove the woody parts with an apple corer. Retain the slices for the garnish.
5. Peel and segment the oranges, mixing any resulting juice with the lemon juice.
6. Retain some orange segments for the garnish, placing the rest into the juice.
7. Wash and peel the apples and pears, remove the cores, then cut into dice and add to the orange segments in the juice.
8. Peel the bananas, slice them and add carefully to the fruit salad.
9. Wash and halve the grapes, remove the pips, and mix into the fruit salad.
10. Flavour the fruit salad with the sugar and maraschino, and allow to stand for 1 hour.

Service:

11. From the fruit salad remove some perfect grape halves and banana slices for the garnish and put to one side.
12. Fill the rest of the fruit salad into the pineapple halves.
13. Arrange the pineapple slices on the left-hand side, overlapping each other.
14. Arrange the orange segments on the right in the same way.
15. Arrange a banana slice in the centre with a grape on top.
16. Arrange the pineapple halves at an angle in two rows on a large platter.

Mangos and Kiwifruit in Pawpaws

To serve 8:

300 ml/11 fl. oz water

100 gr/3½ oz sugar

25 gr/1 oz milk chocolate couverture

25 gr/1 oz plain chocolate couverture

25 gr/1 oz cocoa powder

a little rum if desired

4 pawpaws (papayas)

2 mangos

6 kiwifruit

juice of 1 lemon

20 ml/¾ fl. oz maraschino

some sugar

some water

Time Necessary:

Preparation: 15 minutes
Service: 15 minutes

 Advice

A raspberry or strawberry coulis may be served as a sauce to go with this dish, or may be substituted for the chocolate.

Preparation:

1. Bring the water and sugar to the boil and dissolve the chocolate couverture carefully in it.
2. Add the cocoa powder to the mixture, then carefully bring it all to the boil once only. Allow to cool, stirring from time to time. If desired, the chocolate mixture may be flavoured with a little rum.
3. Halve the pawpaws lengthwise and remove the seeds. Peel the halves and cut a flat on the outside curve, so that they will stand better.
4. Cut the flesh from the mangos in segments and remove from the stone. Remove the peel from the segments.
5. Peel the kiwis and cut them into slices of an even thickness.
6. Mix together the lemon juice, maraschino, sugar and some water.

Service:

7. Lay the mango slices at an angle pointing to the left and slightly overlapping in the pawpaw halves.
8. Lay the kiwi slices on the right-hand side in the same fashion. Sprinkle with the liquor.
9. Pour out a pool of chocolate into the centre of 8 dessert plates, and place the filled pawpaw halves centrally on top.
10. Arrange the plates on a large silver dish and serve.

SAUCES
AND ASPICS

Sauces

Mayonnaise

To serve 8:

4 egg yolks

2 teaspoons mustard

1 teaspoon lemon juice

1 teaspoon cucumber juice

250 ml/9 fl. oz oil

salt, pepper

Time Necessary:

Preparation: 10 minutes

Preparation:

1. Make sure all ingredients are at room temperature. Mix together the egg yolks, mustard, lemon juice and cucumber juice with a whisk.
2. Now beat the mixture until it starts to stiffen, then add the oil, drop by drop.
3. When half the oil is incorporated, the rest may be added quicker.
4. Season the mayonnaise with salt and pepper.

Mayonnaise has a place in the cold kitchen as a basic sauce, and therefore should not be too strongly seasoned. If the mayonnaise is too thick, it may be thinned out with a few drops of water, or a dash of vinegar. If the mayonnaise has separated, beat an egg yolk with a little water, then beat this mixture into the mayonnaise.

Salad Mayonnaise

For 6 Canapés:

about 10 prepared lettuce leaves

2 dessertspoons mayonnaise

1 teaspoon sour cream

salt, pepper

Time Necessary:

Preparation: 10 minutes

Preparation:

1. Cut the lettuce into fine strips.
2. Beat the mayonnaise together with the sour cream to a smooth consistency and season with salt and pepper.
3. Mix the lettuce strips into the sauce. This sauce can be used for canapés (see p. 48 ff.)

Green Sauce

To serve 8:

100 gr/3½ oz fresh spinach

1 bunch parsley

1 bunch chives

250 gr/9 oz mayonnaise

salt, pepper

Time Necessary:

Preparation: 30 minutes

Preparation:

1. Clean, wash and blanch the spinach.
2. Wash the parsley, pull off the stalks and chop the leaves finely.
3. Wash the chives and chop finely.
4. Put the spinach and parsley together with a little water into the liquidiser or food processor and reduce to a purée.
5. Add the chopped chives to the purée and mix into the mayonnaise.
6. Season the sauce with a little salt and pepper.

Green Herb Sauce

To serve 8:

1 pack green herb sauce mixture (if available), otherwise, a mixture of the following herbs: borage, chervil, lovage, parsley, pimpernel, chives, samphire, dill weed

2 hard-boiled eggs

100 gr/3½ oz mayonnaise

125 gr/4 oz sour cream

salt, pepper

mustard, if required

Time Necessary:

Preparation: 20 minutes

Preparation:

1. Clean and wash the herbs then chop them finely.
2. Halve the hard-boiled eggs, separate the whites from the yolks and chop each finely into dice.
3. Mix the mayonnaise and sour cream together smoothly, and add the prepared herbs and eggs.
4. Season with salt and pepper, and a little mustard, if necessary.

Remoulade Sauce

To serve 8:

1 onion

2 small dill pickled cucumbers

1 teaspoon capers

2 anchovy fillets

250 gr/9 oz mayonnaise

1 dessertspoon mustard

1 dessertspoon chopped parsley

salt, pepper

Time Necessary:

Preparation: 20 minutes

Preparation:

1. Peel and chop the onion very finely. Cut the dill pickle into very fine dice. Chop the capers and anchovies finely.
2. Beat the mayonnaise and mustard together.
3. Add the prepared ingredients together with the parsley, and season the made sauce with salt and pepper, if necessary. Should the sauce be made 1 or 2 days before use, reduce the quantity of onion, or else the flavour will be too intense.

Cress and Mustard Sauce

To serve 8:

50 gr/1¾ oz cress

125 gr/4 oz mayonnaise

100 gr/3½ oz mustard

50 gr/1¾ oz cream

some sugar

salt, pepper

Time Necessary:

Preparation: 15 minutes

Preparation:

1. Wash the cress and chop finely. If water cress is used, pull the leaves from the stalks before chopping them.
2. Mix together the mayonnaise, mustard and cream, add the chopped cress and mix well together.
3. Season with a little sugar, salt and pepper.

Mustard and Dill Sauce

To serve 8:

1 bunch dill weed
250 gr/9 oz medium strength mustard
100 gr/3½ oz mayonnaise
100 gr/3½ oz sugar
juice of 1 lemon
salt, pepper

Time Necessary:

Preparation: 15 minutes

Preparation:

1. Wash the dill, remove all coarse stalks and chop finely.
2. Mix the mustard with the mayonnaise and the sugar to a smooth paste, adding a little water, if necessary.
3. Mix in the chopped dill and the lemon juice. Season with salt and pepper, if needed.

Cocktail Sauce

To serve 8:

250 gr/9 oz mayonnaise
juice of 2 lemons
juice of 2 oranges
2 dessertspoons tomato ketchup
1 dessertspoon tomato purée
1 dessertspoon horseradish
40 ml/1½ fl. oz brandy
salt, cayenne pepper

Time Necessary:

Preparation: 20 minutes

Preparation:

1. Mix the mayonnaise together with the orange juice and lemon juice smoothly.
2. Add the tomato ketchup and tomato purée and mix well together.
3. Add the horseradish and mix in well.
4. Season the sauce with the brandy, salt and cayenne pepper to taste.

Tyrolean Sauce

To serve 8:

2 tomatoes
250 gr/9 oz mayonnaise
2 dessertspoons tomato purée
cream or milk, if necessary
2 dessertspoons chopped parsley
salt, pepper

Time Necessary:

Preparation: 20 minutes

Preparation:

1. Wash the tomatoes, remove the stalks and blanch the fruit. Skin, then cut into halves before removing the seeds and thick centre fleshy part.
2. Cut the outside flesh into 5 mm/¼" dice.
3. Mix the mayonnaise smoothly together with the tomato purée, then add the cream or milk to thin slightly.
4. Add the diced tomato to the mixture, and season with salt and pepper.

Chive and Yoghurt Sauce

To serve 8:

2 bunches chives

250 gr/9 oz yoghurt

2 dessertspoons cream

juice of 1 lemon

salt, pepper

Time Necessary:

Preparation: 10 minutes

Preparation:

1. Wash the chives and chop finely.
2. Beat the yoghurt together smoothly with the cream.
3. Add the chives, then season the sauce with salt, pepper and lemon juice.

From this basic sauce a Chervil and Yoghurt Sauce can be produced if the chives are replaced with chervil. The chive and yoghurt sauce can also be improved with the addition of a little chopped chervil, if desired.

Chive Cream Cheese

To serve 8:

1 bunch chives

200 gr/7 oz quark (soft curd cheese)

a little cream

salt, pepper

Time Necessary:

Preparation: 10 minutes

Preparation:

1. Wash and finely chop the chives.
2. Mix the quark together smoothly with the cream.
3. Mix in the chopped chives, then season with salt and pepper.

Chervil Cream

To serve 8:

2 bunches chervil

250 gr/9 oz soured cream (crème fraîche)

200 gr/7 oz cream

salt, pepper

juice of 1 lemon

Time Necessary:

Preparation: 15 minutes

Preparation:

1. Wash the chervil, pull the stalks from the leaves, then chop the leaves finely.
2. Beat the soured cream together with the cream.
3. Mix in the chopped chervil, then season the sauce with salt, pepper and lemon juice.

With all sauces made from a basis of yoghurt or soured cream the flavour can be heightened by the addition of a hint of garlic.

Cress Purée

Preparation:

1. Wash the watercress and pull the leaves from the stalks.
2. Add a little water to the leaves and reduce to a purée in a liquidiser or food processor.
3. Mix the cress purée together with the sour cream and season with the finely chopped garlic, salt and pepper.

Keep a few leaves of watercress back to garnish the dish for which this sauce is intended.

To serve 8:

300 gr/11 oz watercress

150 gr/5½ oz sour cream

1 clove garlic, finely chopped

salt, pepper

Time Necessary:

Preparation: 15 minutes

Egg and Herb Sauce

Preparation:

1. Cut the dill pickled cucumber into fine dice. Peel the onion and cut into dice also.
2. Wash and blanch the tomato. Remove the skin, cut into halves, removing the seeds and core, then cut the flesh into dice.
3. Cut the hard boiled eggs in half, separate the whites from the yolks and chop each, separately, into dice.
4. Mix the vinegar and oil together and mix in all the ingredients one after another, except the eggs.
5. Season with salt and pepper. Add the eggs just before service only.

To serve 8:

2 pickled cucumbers (dill pickles)

1 onion

1 tomato

2 hard boiled eggs

4 dessertspoons vinegar

125 ml/4 fl. oz oil

1 dessertspoon chopped parsley

1 dessertspoon chopped chives

salt, pepper

Time Necessary:

Preparation: 20 minutes

Horseradish Cream

Preparation:

1. Soften the gelatine in cold water, before draining it and gently warming it until it has melted.
2. Wash and peel the horseradish root. Grate it finely, or pass it through the medium plate of a mincing machine (meat grinder).
3. Beat the cream until stiff and add it to the grated horseradish.
4. Add the lemon juice, salt and pepper to taste, with a little sugar, if desired.
5. Beat in the dissolved gelatine quickly.

To produce *Cranberry Horseradish Sauce* beat in some spoonfuls of cooked cranberries.

To serve 8:

2 sheets gelatine

1 root horseradish

125 ml/4 fl. oz cream

juice of 1 lemon

salt, pepper

some sugar

Time Necessary:

Preparation: 20 minutes

Orange Sauce

To serve 8:

4 untreated oranges

250 ml/9 fl. oz fresh orange juice

2 dessertspoons corn flour (corn starch)

40 ml/1½ fl. oz white wine

5 gr/⅙ oz grated ginger

Time Necessary:

Preparation: 20 minutes

Preparation:

1. Wash the oranges and using a julienne cutter (zester), remove the zest from the orange peel.
2. Cook the zest in some orange juice until soft.
3. Mix the corn flour (corn starch) with the white wine.
4. Bring the orange juice to the boil, then add the wine and starch mixture, stirring all the time until it thickens. Allow to get cold.
5. Halve the oranges, cut into segments, saving any resulting juice, and mix with the zest into the prepared sauce.
6. Flavour the sauce with a little grated ginger.

Cumberland Sauce, or Cranberry Sauce

To serve 8:

100 gr/3½ oz cranberry jelly

100 gr/3½ oz red currant jelly

100 ml/3½ fl. oz red wine

1 untreated orange

1 untreated lemon

cayenne pepper

5 gr/⅙ oz English mustard powder

some horseradish

Time Necessary:

Preparation: 20 minutes

Preparation:

1. Wash the orange and lemon, and using a julienne cutter (zester), remove the zest from the orange and lemon peel.
2. Cook the zests in half of the red wine, with a little water.
3. Mix the English mustard with the remaining red wine until smooth, then bring to the boil.
4. Pass the cranberry sauce and red currant jelly through a hair sieve.
5. Halve the orange and lemon, squeeze out the juice and pass this also through the hair sieve, then add to the jelly.
6. Add the orange and lemon zests to the mixture, together with the English mustard and wine, and mix well together.
7. Finally, season with a little cayenne pepper and horseradish to give a piquant flavour.

Poultry Sauce for the Ham Mousse

To make about 1000 ml/35 fl. oz stock:

400 gr/14 oz poultry bones
100 gr/3½ oz veal bones
1 teaspoon salt
100 gr/3½ oz mixed prepared vegetables (leek, celery, carrot)
1500 ml/35 fl. oz water
some parsley

Sauce:

50 gr/1¾ oz butter
60 gr/2 oz flour
100 gr/3½ oz cream
some white wine
salt, pepper

Time Necessary:

Preparation: 3 hours

Preparation:

1. Blanch the chicken and veal bones in boiling water for about 2 minutes.
2. Pour the water away, and rinse off the bones with cold water.
3. Place the bones in a pan with 1500 ml/53 fl. oz cold water and bring to the boil.
4. Remove any scum during cooking.
5. Add salt and just before the end of the cooking period (about 2 hours), add the vegetables.
6. Pass the stock through a cloth on to the parsley and allow to cool.
7. When the stock is cold, remove any fat from the upper surface. This stock may now be frozen in portions if it is not all required at once.
8. Now make the sauce with the stock. Melt the butter in a pan, allow to foam, then add the flour and beat in with a whisk.
9. Fill with the cold stock. Bring to the boil and cook for 20 minutes, stirring constantly.
10. Add the cream and white wine, then season with salt and pepper.
11. While the sauce is cooling, stir from time to time, to prevent a skin from forming.

Aspic

Aspic for Coating Dishes

1000 ml/35 fl. oz water
50 gr/1¾ oz aspic powder

Time Necessary:

Preparation: 10 minutes

Preparation:

1. Bring the water to the boil.
2. Dissolve the aspic powder according to the manufacturer's instructions, and add to the boiling water.
3. Cook the aspic until it is clear. Pass through a cloth and allow to get cold.

Advice

If used to coat silver dishes, use the aspic fairly hot, to avoid premature setting.

Fish Aspic

To produce about
1000 ml/35 fl. oz

500 gr/18 oz fish trimmings, heads and fins etc.

1 onion

1 leek

1 carrot

some celery

2 dessertspoons oil

1 bouquet garni

5 crushed peppercorns

salt

100 gr/3½ oz pike-perch fillet

3 egg whites

100 ml/3½ fl. oz white wine

12 sheets gelatine

Time Necessary:

Preparation: 60 minutes

Preparation:

1. Clean the fish trimmings, ie remove any gills and inner parts.
2. Chop the trimmings roughly and then wash under running water and drain well.
3. Clean the vegetables and cut into slices.
4. Heat the oil in a high sided pan.
5. Sweat off the fish trimmings and vegetables and fill with 1500 ml/53 fl. oz water.
6. Bring to the boil, skimming any albumen from the top while cooking.
7. Add the bouquet garni and the peppercorns together with a little salt.
8. Let the stock simmer lightly for about 20 minutes.
9. Pass the stock through a cloth and allow to cool.
10. Remove any fat from the top surface.
11. The stock must now be clarified, so that the aspic will be clear. Chop the pike-perch fillet and add it to the egg white. Beat this mixture together with a whisk, and pour it into a high-sided pan.
12. Pour over the cold stock, beating all the time and bring to the boil, while still beating.
13. When the egg white sets, stop beating and allow the stock to stand for about 15 minutes.
14. Pass the stock through a cloth and add the white wine. Mix in the dissolved gelatine and allow the aspic to cool ready for further use.

Meat Aspic

To produce about
1500 ml/53 fl. oz

250 gr/9 oz veal bones

250 gr/9 oz beef bones

1 teaspoon salt, 1 onion

100 gr/3½ oz mixed prepared vegetables

some parsley

150 gr/5¼ oz lean beef/3 egg whites

40 ml/1½ fl. oz madeira

12 sheets gelatine

salt, pepper

Time Necessary:

Preparation: 3 hours

Preparation:

1. Blanch the veal and beef bones briefly in boiling water.
2. Pour away the water and rinse off the bones.
3. Put the bones into a pan with 2000 ml/70 fl. oz of water and bring to the boil, skimming carefully to remove all scum.
4. Peel the onion, cut in half and brown off the cut side in a hot, dry pan.
5. Add the vegetables and the browned onion to the stock and cook it out for 2 hours.
6. Pass the stock through a cloth on to the parsley and allow to get cold. Remove any fat from the top surface.
7. The stock must now be clarified. Chop the meat up finely and add to the egg whites. Beat together briefly with a whisk, and put into a high-sided pot.
8. As soon as the clarifying meat floats on the surface, stop stirring, and cook on for a further 15 minutes.
9. Pass through a cloth, add the madeira and the softened gelatine.
10. Season, if necessary, with salt and pepper and place in a cool place for later use.

Notes on use of leaf gelatine

1. Leaf gelatine must be thoroughly soaked in cold water before use.
2. The sheets of gelatine must be put into the water individually.
3. After soaking, the gelatine must be well drained. If to be used in hot sauces or liquids, it may be dissolved directly in the liquid.
4. If the gelatine is to be used in cold sauces or for salads, then it must be melted over low heat and then added to the liquid quickly, stirring all the time, in order to avoid the formation of lumps.

Index of Recipes